100
Sweets & Candies

100
Sweets & Candies

Edited by
Jo Barker

octopus

Contents

NOTES
Standard spoon measurements are used in all recipes
1 tablespoon = one 15 ml spoon
1 teaspoon = one 5 ml spoon
All spoon measures are level.

For all recipes, quantities are given in metric, imperial and American measures. Follow one set of measures only, because they are not interchangeable.
Ovens should always be preheated to the specified temperature.

First published 1983 by
Octopus Books Limited
59 Grosvenor Street, London W1

© 1983 Octopus Books Limited

ISBN 0 7064 1951 0

Produced by Mandarin Publishers Ltd
22a Westlands Rd
Quarry Bay, Hong Kong

Printed in Hong Kong

Frontispiece: a selection of homemade sweets and candies (Photograph: Kraft Foods)

Introduction

Homemade sweets and candies are easy to make and delicious to eat. The recipes in this book offer plenty of scope for creative and culinary skills for all abilities and all ages. Indeed many of these recipes are suitable for children to prepare with the minimum of supervision. They'll have fun making the candies plus a tasty end result for the family as well.

Most of the recipes use normal kitchen equipment and basic store cupboard ingredients which means they could turn a dull rainy day into an exciting time spent shaping and colouring candies to produce mouthwatering results. Some of the sweets and candies are quick and easy to make like marzipan, others such as toffee require more skill and patience to achieve a good result. If you are a beginner, choose the simple uncooked recipes first and work up to those requiring more skill so as not to be disappointed when you try a difficult recipe and fail to achieve the results you were anticipating.

For the fudge and toffee recipes, a sugar thermometer will be a great asset for constant success. Remember to stand the sugar thermometer in warm water before use. If a cold thermometer is plunged into the boiling syrup, it will crack or the glass may break. The bulb of the thermometer must be fully immersed for an accurate reading of the temperature. Clean the thermometer in hot water, making sure the sugar has dissolved, then dry and store it carefully. Always use a good heavy-based pan for these recipes.

When making toffee or boiled sweets, beware of the bubbling boiling syrup as it can give a nasty burn so never be tempted to dip your finger in for a taste. If you are working toffee or boiled mixtures, take care not to melt the laminated work surface — a marble slab is the perfect answer but a very well oiled wooden board works well too.

If you do not have a sugar thermometer, use the following tests for the different stages in sugar boiling:

Soft ball (113-117°C/235-243°F) — for fondants and fudges. Drop some syrup into cold water, when rolled between the fingers, it should form a soft ball.

Hard ball (118-130°C/245-265°F) — for nougats and marshmallows. Drop some syrup into cold water, the ball which forms should hold its shape.

Soft crack (132-143°C/270-290°F) — for toffee. Drop some syrup into cold water, it will separate into hard but not brittle threads.

Hard crack (149-154°C/300-310°F) — for hard toffees. Drop some syrup into cold water, it will separate into hard brittle threads.

Caramel (156°C/313°F) — for caramels. The colour of the syrup changes from golden brown to dark brown.

All sorts of sugars

Sugar or the alternative sweetener, honey, is the basic ingredient of these sweets and candies. The various sugars available contribute to the variety of flavours and textures. Preserving or lump sugar gives the cleanest scum-free syrup. Granulated sugar gives a gritty texture. Caster sugar has very fine crystals and dissolves very quickly. Icing (confectioners') sugar gives a smooth texture. Natural brown sugars contribute flavour as well as sweetness. There are several natural brown sugars which come from Barbados, Guyana or Mauritius. Demerara sugar has clear sparkling crystals of large consistent size and a sticky texture. Light brown or muscovado sugar is a soft, smaller crystal with a mild flavour. Dark brown sugar, Barbados or muscovado is dark and sticky with a light toffee flavour. Molasses sugar is soft and almost black with a treacle toffee flavour.

Sweets and candies do not have to be expensive to look appetising and taste delicious. Some of the recipes are for small quantities enough to satisfy your sweet tooth and creative instinct but not too much to add inches to your waistline!

When you are making a larger quantity of sweets and candies than you will eat immediately, take trouble with the packing and storing. A general rule is to store them in airtight containers in a cool place, especially the chocolate ones. Wrap each sweet or candy individually or place in a paper sweet case before packing close enough together to prevent movement but not to squash each other.

Homemade candies make a super present for a friend or relation. Consider the overall effect of colour and shape when packing the sweets and candies — they will taste even better if they are attractively displayed. Boxes in all shapes, colours and sizes are now available in shops or you can simply decorate an empty box you already have at home. Cover the candies with cling film (plastic wrap) to prevent them absorbing other smells and if they are a present, add a pretty bow as well.

Marzipan Sweets & Candies

Marzipan (almond paste) is delicious whether made at home or bought in packets. It can be used for all kinds of sweets and candies or just simply coloured to make pretty marzipan fruits. When making your own marzipan, vary the flavour by using white or brown sugar and adding different essences and liqueurs. If the mixture is too sticky, sprinkle the work surface with sifted icing (confectioners') sugar.

Muscovado Marzipan Candies

METRIC/IMPERIAL
Light marzipan:
100 g/4 oz ground
    almonds
50 g/2 oz light
    muscovado sugar
50 g/2 oz icing sugar,
    sieved
squeeze of lemon
    juice
1 drop vanilla essence
2 drops almond
    essence
2 tablespoons beaten
    egg
Dark marzipan:
1 tablespoon cocoa
    powder
1 teaspoon hot water
100 g/4 oz ground
    almonds
100 g/4 oz dark
    muscovado sugar
100 g/4 oz icing sugar,
    sieved
½ teaspoon vanilla
    essence
squeeze of lemon
    juice
3 tablespoons beaten
    egg

AMERICAN
Light marzipan:
1 cup ground
    almonds
⅓ cup light brown
    sugar
½ cup sifted confec-
    tioners' sugar
squeeze of lemon
    juice
1 drop vanilla
2 drops almond
    extract
2 tablespoons beaten
    egg
Dark marzipan:
1 tablespoon
    unsweetened cocoa
    powder
1 teaspoon hot water
1 cup ground
    almonds
⅔ cup dark brown
    sugar
1 cup sifted confec-
    tioners' sugar
½ teaspoon vanilla
squeeze of lemon
    juice
3 tablespoons beaten
    egg

To make the light marzipan: mix the ground almonds, sugars, lemon juice, vanilla, almond essence (extract), with enough of the beaten egg to make a manageable paste.

To make the dark marzipan: blend the cocoa with the hot water and mix together with the remaining ingredients to make a manageable paste.

You can now use the marzipans to make these different candies.

Almond candies: shape the marzipan into almond shapes. Top the dark marzipan with blanched almonds and the light marzipan with unblanched almonds. Place in paper sweet (candy) cases.

Pinwheels: form some light marzipan into a long, thin "sausage" shape. Roll out two strips of marzipan, making the light marzipan slightly wider than the dark. Wrap the dark marzipan around the "sausage" shape and the other light marzipan around the outside. Cut the roll into 5 mm (¼ inch) wide slices.

Stripy candies: roll out three strips of light and three strips of dark marzipan about 20 × 5 cm (8 × 2 inches) wide. Lay these pieces, alternating the colours, on top of each other. Cut into four long strips and then cut each of these strips into 6 pieces.

Muscovado Marzipan Candies
(Photograph: Billingtons Natural Unrefined Sugars)

Marzipan Fruits

METRIC/IMPERIAL	AMERICAN
450 g/1 lb ground almonds	4 cups ground almonds
225 g/8 oz caster sugar	1 cup firmly packed sugar
225 g/8 oz icing sugar, sieved	1¾ cups sifted confectioners' sugar
2 tablespoons lemon juice	2 tablespoons lemon juice
1 tablespoon brandy	1 tablespoon brandy
1 tablespoon orange flower water	1 tablespoon orange flavored extract
½ teaspoon vanilla essence	½ teaspoon vanilla extract
4 drops almond essence	4 drops almond extract
1 large egg, beaten	1 large egg, beaten
Decoration:	**Decoration:**
orange, yellow, green, red and brown food colourings	orange, yellow, green, red and brown food colorings
cloves	cloves
angelica	angelica

Place the ground almonds, sugars, lemon juice, brandy, orange flower water (orange flavored extract), vanilla and almond essences (extracts) in a bowl. Mix to a manageable paste with enough of the egg. Turn onto a work surface sprinkled with icing (confectioners') sugar and knead until smooth.

Oranges – colour some of the paste orange. Roll into balls on a fine grater. Insert a clove at one end and toss in sugar.

Lemons – colour some of the paste yellow. Roll into ovals on a fine grater, pinch one end to a point and put a clove in the other end. Roll the lemons in sugar.

Apples – colour some of the paste green. Roll into balls and insert a stalk of angelica. Paint one side a rosy red.

Pears – colour some of the paste green or yellow. Roll into pear shapes and insert a clove at one end.

Strawberries – colour some of the paste red. Roll into strawberry shapes. Make an angelica hull and toss the strawberries in sugar.

Bananas – colour some of the paste yellow. Roll and curve into banana shapes. Use brown food colouring to make skin markings.

Place the fruits in paper sweet (candy) cases and leave overnight before packing in an airtight container.

Almond Candies

METRIC/IMPERIAL	AMERICAN
225 g/8 oz ground almonds	2 cups ground almonds
100 g/4 oz caster sugar	½ cup sugar
100 g/4 oz icing sugar, sieved	1 scant cup sifted confectioners' sugar
1 tablespoon Cointreau	1 tablespoon Cointreau
1 egg, beaten	1 egg, beaten
50 g/2 oz seedless raisins	⅓ cup seedless raisins
Decoration:	**Decoration:**
25 g/1 oz icing sugar, sieved	¼ cup sifted confectioners' sugar
75 g/3 oz plain chocolate, broken into pieces	3 squares (1 oz each) semi-sweet chocolate, broken into pieces
6 coloured glacé cherries, cut into 18 pieces	6 colored glacé cherries, cut into 18 pieces

Place the ground almonds, sugars and liqueur in a bowl. Mix to a manageable paste with enough of the egg. Knead in the raisins. Shape into 18 balls and dust with icing (confectioners') sugar.

Melt the chocolate in a bowl over a pan of hot water or in a double boiler. Remove from the heat. Dip the top halves of the candies into the chocolate. Put in paper sweet (candy) cases, chocolate end up, and place a piece of cherry on each one.

Makes 18

Illustrated on page 46

8

Crunchy Delights

METRIC/IMPERIAL	AMERICAN
50 g/2 oz ground almonds	½ cup ground almonds
50 g/2 oz caster sugar	¼ cup sugar
50 g/2 oz icing sugar, sieved	½ cup sifted confectioners' sugar
1 teaspoon lemon juice	1 teaspoon lemon juice
1 egg yolk	1 egg yolk
25 g/1 oz glacé cherries, chopped	3 tablespoons chopped glacé cherries
25 g/1 oz walnuts, chopped	¼ cup chopped walnuts
6 level tablespoons Coco Krispies cereal	6 tablespoons Coco Krispies cereal

Place the ground almonds, sugars and lemon juice in a bowl. Mix to a manageable paste with enough of the egg yolk. Knead in the cherries and walnuts and shape into 18 balls.

Roll each ball in the cereal to coat completely then place in paper sweet (candy) cases.
Makes 18

Fairy Mushrooms

METRIC/IMPERIAL	AMERICAN
50 g/2 oz ground almonds	½ cup ground almonds
25 g/1 oz caster sugar	2 tablespoons sugar
25 g/1 oz icing sugar, sieved	¼ cup sifted confectioners' sugar
1 drop almond essence	1 drop almond extract
½ small egg yolk	½ small egg yolk
25 g/1 oz chocolate	1 square (1 oz) chocolate
3 tablespoons puffed rice cereal	3 tablespoons puffed rice cereal

Place the ground almonds and sugars into a bowl with the almond essence (extract). Mix to a manageable paste with the egg yolk. Shape into 12 small "sausage" shapes with one end slightly wider than the other.

Melt the chocolate in a bowl over a pan of hot water or in a double boiler. Remove from the heat. Dip the narrower ends of the "sausages" into the chocolate and then into the cereal. Stand the mushrooms on their wider ends.
Makes 12

Marzipan Walnuts

METRIC/IMPERIAL	AMERICAN
100 g/4 oz ground almonds	1 cup ground almonds
50 g/2 oz light muscovado sugar	⅓ cup light brown sugar
50 g/2 oz icing sugar, sieved	½ cup sifted confectioners' sugar
1 drop vanilla essence	1 drop vanilla
2 drops almond essence	2 drops almond extract
1 tablespoon cocoa powder	1 tablespoon unsweetened cocoa powder
2 teaspoons hot water	2 teaspoons hot water
1 egg, beaten	1 egg, beaten
10 walnut halves	10 walnut halves

Place the ground almonds, sugars, vanilla and almond essences (extracts) into a bowl. Mix the cocoa powder to a paste with the hot water and add to the almond mixture. Mix to a manageable paste with enough of the egg.

Turn the paste onto a work surface sprinkled with icing (confectioners') sugar and knead until smooth. Roll out the paste and cut out 10 circles using a 2.5 cm (1 inch) fluted cutter. Press half a walnut in each circle and place in paper sweet (candy) cases.
Makes 10

Stuffed Dates

METRIC/IMPERIAL	AMERICAN
100 g/4 oz ground almonds	1 cup ground almonds
50 g/2 oz caster sugar	¼ cup sugar
50 g/2 oz icing sugar, sieved	½ cup sifted confectioners' sugar
1 teaspoon lemon juice	1 teaspoon lemon juice
2 teaspoons orange flower water	2 teaspoons orange flavored extract
1 tablespoon brandy	1 tablespoon brandy
1 egg, beaten	1 egg, beaten
food colouring of your choice	food coloring of your choice
20 stoned dates	20 pitted dates

Place the ground almonds, sugars, lemon juice, orange flower water (orange flavored extract) and brandy in a bowl. Mix to a manageable paste with the egg and add food colouring of your choice. Knead the almond paste until smooth.

Fill the dates with the almond paste and place in paper sweet (candy) cases.
Makes 20

Surprise Squares

METRIC/IMPERIAL	AMERICAN
75 g/3 oz butter	¼ cup plus 2 tablespoons butter
75 g/3 oz soft light brown sugar	½ cup firmly packed light brown sugar
1 egg, lightly beaten	1 egg, lightly beaten
65 g/2½ oz self-raising flour	½ cup plus 2 tablespoons self-rising flour
1 tablespoon cocoa powder	1 tablespoon unsweetened cocoa powder
25 g/1 oz walnuts, chopped	¼ cup chopped walnuts
25 g/1 oz stoned dates, chopped	3 tablespoons pitted and chopped dates
50 g/2 oz glacé cherries, chopped	¼ cup chopped glacé cherries
175 g/6 oz marzipan	6 oz almond paste
icing sugar to decorate	confectioners' sugar to decorate

Cream together the butter and brown sugar. Beat in the egg and fold in the sieved flour and cocoa using a metal spoon. Spread half of this mixture into a greased and base lined 18 cm (7 inch) square tin (pan). Sprinkle the nuts, dates and cherries onto the mixture.

Roll out the marzipan (almond paste) to an 18 cm (7 inch) square and lay it over the fruit and nuts in the tin. Spread the remaining cake mixture evenly on top.

Cook in a preheated moderate oven (180°C/350°F, Gas Mark 4) for 35 to 40 minutes. Leave to cool in the tin. Cut into 49 squares when cold. Decorate the squares by sprinkling icing (confectioners') sugar over stencil shapes to give a pretty effect.
Makes 49

Surprise Squares
(Photograph: Cadbury Typhoo Food Advisory Service)

Almond Melties

METRIC/IMPERIAL	AMERICAN
1 egg white	1 egg white
50 g/2 oz ground almonds	½ cup ground almonds
25 g/1 oz caster sugar	2 tablespoons sugar
2-3 drops almond essence	2-3 drops almond extract
Decoration:	**Decoration:**
glacé cherries	glacé cherries
angelica	angelica

Line a baking sheet with rice paper.

Whisk the egg white in a deep bowl and fold in the ground almonds, sugar and almond essence (extract). Spoon the mixture into a piping (pastry) bag with a star nozzle attached. Pipe 15 stars onto the rice paper and cook in a preheated moderate oven (180°C/350°F, Gas Mark 4) for 10 to 15 minutes.

Decorate each candy with a tiny piece of cherry and angelica and leave until cold.
Makes 15

Ginger Triangles

METRIC/IMPERIAL	AMERICAN
225 g/8 oz ground almonds	2 cups ground almonds
100 g/4 oz light muscovado sugar	⅔ cup light brown sugar
100 g/4 oz icing sugar, sieved	1 scant cup sifted confectioners' sugar
1 teaspoon lemon juice	1 teaspoon lemon juice
½ teaspoon vanilla essence	½ teaspoon vanilla
1 teaspoon orange flower water	1 teaspoon orange flavored extract
finely grated rind and juice of 1 orange	finely grated rind and juice of 1 orange
2 eggs, beaten	2 eggs, beaten
100 g/4 oz crystallized ginger, chopped	⅔ cup chopped candied ginger
orange food colouring	orange food coloring

Place the ground almonds, sugars, lemon juice, vanilla, orange flower water (orange flavored extract) and orange juice in a bowl. Add enough of the egg to make a manageable paste and divide the mixture in half. Knead the chopped ginger into one half of the almond paste and shape into a 2.5 cm (1 inch) triangular bar.

Knead the finely grated orange rind and food colouring into the remaining half of almond paste. Roll out to a rectangle the same length as the bar and 7.5 cm (3 inches) wide. Wrap the orange almond paste around the ginger bar, keeping the triangular bar shape and seal the edge. Cut into 1 cm (½ inch) slices.
Makes about 30

Chocolate and Almond Squares

METRIC/IMPERIAL	AMERICAN
50 g/2 oz plain chocolate, broken into pieces	2 squares (1 oz each) semi-sweet chocolate, broken into pieces
100 g/4 oz ground almonds	1 cup ground almonds
50 g/2 oz full fat soft cheese	¼ cup full fat soft cheese
15 g/½ oz icing sugar, sieved	2 tablespoons sifted confectioners' sugar
finely grated rind of 1 orange	finely grated rind of 1 orange

Melt the chocolate in a bowl over a pan of hot water or in a double boiler. Stir in half the ground almonds and remove from the heat. Chill.

Cream the cheese and sugar together. Gradually work in the remaining almonds and orange rind.

Place the chocolate mixture between two sheets of greaseproof (waxed) paper and roll out to a 23 × 18 cm (9 × 7 inch) rectangle. Repeat with the orange mixture. Peel the paper off the top of both mixtures and turn the orange mixture over onto the chocolate. Trim the edges to form a neat rectangle. Cut the rectangle in half widthways and put one half on top of the other to form 4 layers. Cut into 36 pieces and place in paper cases. Chill.
Makes 36

Brandied Cherries

METRIC/IMPERIAL	AMERICAN
20 glacé cherries (red, green and yellow)	20 glacé cherries (red, green and yellow)
4 tablespoons brandy	¼ cup brandy
225 g/8 oz ground almonds	2 cups ground almonds
100 g/4 oz caster sugar	½ cup sugar
100 g/4 oz icing sugar, sieved	1 scant cup sifted confectioners' sugar
1 tablespoon lemon juice	1 tablespoon lemon juice
2 drops vanilla essence	2 drops vanilla
1 drop almond essence	1 drop almond extract
1 teaspoon orange flower water	1 teaspoon orange flavored extract
1 egg, beaten	1 egg, beaten

Soak the cherries in the brandy for at least an hour. Drain the cherries and reserve the brandy.

Place the ground almonds, sugars, lemon juice, vanilla and almond essences (extracts) and orange flower water (orange flavored extract) in a bowl. Mix to a manageable paste with enough of the egg and brandy to taste. Divide the almond paste into 20 pieces and mould a piece around each cherry. Cut each one in half and place in 40 paper sweet (candy) cases.
Makes 40

Moulded Marzipan

METRIC/IMPERIAL	AMERICAN
450 g/1 lb lump sugar	2 cups cube sugar
150 ml/¼ pint water	⅔ cup water
¼ level teaspoon cream of tartar, dissolved in 1 teaspoon water	¼ teaspoon cream of tartar, dissolved in 1 teaspoon water
350 g/12 oz ground almonds	3 cups ground almonds
2 egg whites	2 egg whites
50 g/2 oz icing sugar, sieved	½ cup sifted confectioners' sugar
2-3 drops almond essence	2-3 drops almond extract

Place the sugar and water in a pan and dissolve the sugar over a gentle heat. Bring the syrup to the boil and stir in the cream of tartar. Boil to the soft ball stage (114°C/238°F). Remove from the heat and beat with a wooden spoon until the syrup becomes cloudy.

Stir in the ground almonds and egg whites. Return the pan to the heat for a few minutes, stirring continuously. Pour the almond mixture onto a work surface and gradually work in the icing (confectioners') sugar and almond essence (extract) with a palette knife. Chill the mixture. Knead and add more icing (confectioners') sugar if necessary.

Mould the almond paste into animal or flower shapes to serve as individual candies or as cake decorations.

Jellies, Marshmallows & Coconut Ice

Tempting jellies and Turkish delight are set with gelatine and can be made in a variety of colours and flavours. Marshmallows and coconut ice are both easy to make at home and taste so delicious that they will disappear as fast as you make them!

Lemon and Eucalyptus Jubes

METRIC/IMPERIAL
3 teaspoons gelatine
120 ml/4 fl oz hot water
120 ml/4 fl oz lemon juice
¾ teaspoon liquid sweetener
⅛ teaspoon citric acid
5 drops eucalyptus oil

AMERICAN
1 envelope unflavored gelatin
½ cup hot water
½ cup lemon juice
¾ teaspoon liquid sweetener
⅛ teaspoon citric acid
5 drops eucalyptus oil

Dissolve the gelatine in the hot water. Stir in the lemon juice, sweetener, citric acid and eucalyptus oil. Pour into a 15 cm (6 inch) square tin and chill until set.

Dip the base of the tin quickly in hot water and invert the mixture on to greaseproof (waxed) paper sprinkled with sugar. Cut into 16 squares with scissors or a hot, damp, sharp knife. Leave plain or toss in sugar.
Makes 16
Variation:
Lime Jubes — use lime instead of the lemon juice and add about 5 drops of green food colouring instead of the eucalyptus oil.

Raspberry Jubes

METRIC/IMPERIAL
3 teaspoons gelatine
120 ml/4 fl oz hot water
1 packet diabetic raspberry jelly
5 drops liquid sweetener
⅛ teaspoon citric acid

AMERICAN
1 envelope unflavored gelatin
½ cup hot water
1 package raspberry-flavored diabetic gelatin
5 drops liquid sweetener
⅛ teaspoon citric acid

Dissolve the gelatine in half of the hot water. Dissolve the jelly (gelatin) in the remaining hot water. Mix the two liquids together. Stir in the sweetener and citric acid.

Pour into a 15 cm (6 inch) square tin (pan) and chill. Cut into 16 cubes and place in paper cases.
Makes 16

Clockwise from back: an assortment of jelly jubes; Coconut Marshmallows (page 17); Milk Chocolate Fudge (page 37); Coconut Ice (Photograph: Davis Gelatine)

Rose and Peppermint Marshmallows

METRIC/IMPERIAL	AMERICAN
450 g/1 lb caster sugar	2 cups sugar
25 g/1 oz golden syrup	1½ tablespoons light corn syrup
300 ml/½ pint hot water	1¼ cups hot water
2 tablespoons gelatine	2 tablespoons unflavored gelatin
2 egg whites	2 egg whites
½ teaspoon peppermint essence	½ teaspoon peppermint extract
few drops of green food colouring	few drops of green food coloring
½ teaspoon rose water	½ teaspoon rose water
few drops of pink food colouring	few drops of pink food coloring
To finish:	**To finish:**
50 g/2 oz icing sugar	½ cup confectioners' sugar
25 g/1 oz cornflour	¼ cup cornstarch

Place the sugar, syrup and 150 ml/¼ pint (⅔ cup) of the water in a large pan and heat gently until sugar has dissolved. Bring to the boil and boil to the hard ball stage (130°C/265°F). Sprinkle the gelatine over the remaining hot water and stir until dissolved. Remove the syrup from the heat and stir in the gelatine.

Whisk the egg whites in a deep bowl. Pour the hot syrup onto the egg whites in a thin stream, whisking all the time until very thick and stiff. Place half the mixture in a separate bowl and add the peppermint essence and green food colouring. Pour into an 18 cm (7 inch) square tin (pan) lined with non-stick (parchment) paper.

Flavour the remaining mixture with the rose water and colour it pale pink. Pour into another 18 cm (7 inch) square tin (pan) lined with non-stick (parchment) paper. Leave both tins exposed to the air for at least 24 hours, then cut into 25 cubes.

Sift together the icing (confectioners') sugar and cornflour (cornstarch) and toss the marshmallows in it. Place in paper sweet (candy) cases.
Makes 50

Lemon Jellies

METRIC/IMPERIAL	AMERICAN
25 g/1 oz gelatine	4 envelopes unflavored gelatin
300 ml/½ pint hot water	1¼ cups hot water
450 g/1 lb caster sugar	2 cups sugar
¼ teaspoon citric acid	¼ teaspoon citric acid
few drops of lemon essence	few drops of lemon extract
few drops of yellow food colouring	few drops of yellow food coloring
sugar to finish	sugar to finish

Dissolve the gelatine in the hot water. Pour into an 18 cm (7 inch) base diameter saucepan with the sugar and citric acid. Stir over a gentle heat until the sugar has completely dissolved. Bring to the boil and boil gently for 20 minutes, stirring occasionally.

Remove from the heat and stir in the lemon flavouring and colouring. Skim off the foam. Pour into a greased 18 cm (7 inch) square tin (pan) and chill overnight.

Loosen the edges with a warm knife and invert on to sugared paper. Cut into 25 cubes with scissors and toss in sugar. Place in paper sweet (candy) cases and leave to dry before storing.
Makes about 25

Pineapple Marshmallows

METRIC/IMPERIAL	AMERICAN
4 teaspoons gelatine	1⅓ envelopes unflavored gelatin
1 packet pineapple jelly	1 package pineapple-flavored gelatin
120 ml/4 fl oz hot water	½ cup hot water
120 ml/4 fl oz fresh orange juice	½ cup fresh orange juice
1 egg white	1 egg white

Dissolve the gelatine and pineapple jelly (gelatin) in the hot water. Stir in the orange juice and whisk until frothy. Leave to chill but not set.

Whisk the egg white until stiff but not dry and fold it into the pineapple mixture. Pour into a 15 cm (6 inch) square tin (pan) and chill until set. Cut into 16 squares.
Note: Pineapple Marshmallows should be eaten on the day they are made.

Plum Jellies

METRIC/IMPERIAL
450 g/1 lb plums
150 ml/¼ pint cold
  water
350 g/12 oz caster
  sugar
3 tablespoons
  gelatine
2 tablespoons hot
  water
sugar to finish

AMERICAN
4 cups plums
⅔ cup cold water
1½ cups sugar
3 tablespoons
  unflavored gelatin
2 tablespoons hot
  water
sugar to finish

Place the plums and cold water in a pan and cook until soft. Discard the stones (pits) and liquidise the plums or rub through a sieve to make a purée. Measure the purée and make it up to 750 ml/1¼ pints (3 cups) with water if necessary.

Place the purée and sugar in an 18 cm (7 inch) base diameter saucepan. Stir over a gentle heat to dissolve the sugar. Dissolve the gelatine in the hot water and stir into the plum mixture. Bring to the boil and boil gently for 45 minutes. Pour into a greased 15 cm (6 inch) square tin (pan) and chill overnight.

Loosen the edges with a warm knife and invert on to sugared paper. Cut into 36 cubes with scissors and toss in sugar. Place in paper sweet (candy) cases and leave to dry before storing.
Makes 36

Coconut Marshmallows

METRIC/IMPERIAL
4 teaspoons gelatine
280 ml/9 fl oz hot
  water
375 g/13 oz caster
  sugar
1 teaspoon vanilla
  essence
75 g/3 oz desiccated
  coconut, toasted

AMERICAN
4 teaspoons
  unflavored gelatin
1 cup plus 2
  tablespoons hot
  water
1⅔ cups sugar
1 teaspoon vanilla
1 cup shredded
  coconut, toasted

Sprinkle the gelatine over the hot water and stir until dissolved. Pour into a deep bowl. Dissolve the sugar and vanilla in the gelatine mixture, stirring continuously. Whisk vigorously until the mixture is white, fluffy and has at least doubled in bulk.

When the mixture thickens, pour it into a greased 18 cm (7 inch) square tin (pan) and chill overnight. Cut into 36 squares and roll in the coconut. Place the marshmallows in paper sweet (candy) cases.
Makes 36
Illustrated on page 14

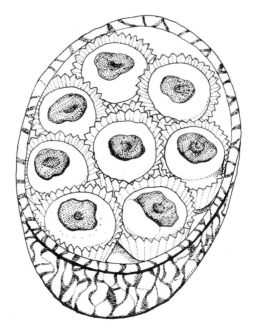

Coconut Ice

METRIC/IMPERIAL	AMERICAN
450 g/1 lb granulated sugar	2 cups sugar
150 ml/¼ pint milk	⅔ cup milk
150 g/5 oz desiccated coconut	1⅔ cups shredded coconut
few drops of pink food colouring	few drops of pink food coloring

Dissolve the sugar in the milk in a deep pan over a gentle heat. Bring to the boil and boil for 10 to 15 minutes to the soft ball stage (114°C/238°F).

Remove the pan from the heat and stir in the coconut. Pour half the mixture into a well greased 15 cm (6 inch) square tin (pan). Quickly colour the remaining half pink and pour it over the white layer. Smooth over the top and leave the coconut ice to cool. When it is half set, mark into 36 squares. Remove from the tin when cold.
Makes 36

Top Hats

METRIC/IMPERIAL	AMERICAN
100 g/4 oz plain chocolate, broken into pieces	4 squares (1 oz each) semisweet chocolate
12 marshmallows	12 marshmallows
12 Smarties	12 Smarties

Place the chocolate in a heatproof bowl over a pan of simmering water until melted. Pour the chocolate into 12 paper cake cases. Place a marshmallow on each and top with a Smartie, attached with a little melted chocolate.

Chill the candies and peel away the paper cases before serving.
Makes 12

Turkish Delight

METRIC/IMPERIAL	AMERICAN
25 g/1 oz gelatine	4 envelopes unflavored gelatin
300 ml/½ pint hot water	1¼ cups hot water
450 g/1 lb caster sugar	2 cups sugar
¼ teaspoon citric acid	¼ teaspoon citric acid
1 tablespoon rose water	1 tablespoon rose water
few drops of pink food colouring	few drops of pink food coloring
To finish:	**To finish:**
25 g/1 oz icing sugar, sieved	2 tablespoons sifted confectioners' sugar
25 g/1 oz cornflour, sieved	¼ cup cornstarch

Sprinkle the gelatine over the hot water and stir until dissolved. Pour into an 18 cm (7 inch) base diameter pan with the sugar and citric acid. Stir over a gentle heat until the sugar has completely dissolved. Bring to the boil and boil gently for 20 minutes, stirring occasionally.

Remove from the heat and stir in the rose water. Whisk the mixture lightly until milky in appearance and pour half into a greased 18 cm (7 inch) square tin (pan). Stand the tin in cold water. Colour the remaining mixture pale pink, whisk lightly and pour over the white layer. Chill for 24 hours.

Sprinkle the icing (confectioners') sugar and cornflour (cornstarch) onto waxed paper. Invert the Turkish Delight onto the paper. Cut into 36 squares with scissors and toss in the sugar mixture.
Makes 36
Variation:
Green food colouring and peppermint flavouring may be used instead of the rose water and pink colouring. Another delicious idea is to add 50 g/2 oz (½ cup) chopped nuts to the mixture. Or the Turkish Delight may be left plain and just flavoured with almond essence.

Coconut Ice; Chocolate and Cherry Fudge (page 33); Turkish Delight; Cinnamon Cushions (page 26) (Photograph: British Sugar Bureau)

Quick Coconut Ice

METRIC/IMPERIAL	AMERICAN
75 g/3 oz full fat soft cheese	1/3 cup full fat soft cheese
1 tablespoon milk	1 tablespoon milk
275 g/10 oz icing sugar, sieved	2 1/4 cups sifted confectioners' sugar
100 g/4 oz desiccated coconut	1 1/3 cups shredded coconut
few drops of pink food colouring	few drops of pink food coloring
25 g/1 oz chocolate	1 square (1 oz) chocolate

Cream the cheese until smooth and beat in the milk. Gradually work in the sugar and coconut. Divide the mixture in half, colour one portion pink and press into a greased 15 cm (6 inch) square tin.

Melt the chocolate in a bowl over a pan of hot water or in a double boiler. Remove from the heat. Work the chocolate into the remaining coconut mixture. Press the chocolate coconut ice on top of the pink layer. Chill for at least 1 hour then cut into 12 bars.
Makes 12 bars

West Country Coconut Ice

METRIC/IMPERIAL	AMERICAN
225 g/8 oz granulated sugar	1 cup sugar
6 tablespoons cider	6 tablespoons cider
100 g/4 oz desiccated coconut	1 1/3 cups shredded coconut
pink food colouring	pink food coloring

Dissolve the sugar in the cider in a pan over a gentle heat. Bring to the boil and boil for 4 minutes. Remove the pan from the heat and stir in the coconut. Spoon half the mixture into a greased 15 cm (6 inch) square tin (pan).

Colour the remaining mixture pink and spoon over the white layer. Smooth over the top and leave to cool. Mark the coconut ice into bars when half set. Remove from the tin when cold.
Makes about 24

Marshmallows

METRIC/IMPERIAL	AMERICAN
2 tablespoons gelatine	2 tablespoons gelatin
120 ml/4 fl oz hot water	1/2 cup hot water
120 ml/4 fl oz cold water	1/2 cup cold water
250 g/9 oz sugar	1 cup sugar
1/8 teaspoon cream of tartar	1/8 teaspoon cream of tartar
1 tablespoon lemon juice	1 tablespoon lemon juice
pinch of salt	pinch of salt

Sprinkle the gelatine over the hot water and stir briskly with a fork until dissolved.

Place the gelatine in a pan with all the remaining ingredients. Boil for 20 minutes until the mixture forms a thread when dropped from a spoon. Stir occasionally while cooking. Remove from the heat and pour the mixture into a heatproof bowl.

Beat the mixture thoroughly until it is thick and white. (An electric mixer is quickest, but a hand beater also gives a good result).

Pour the mixture into a shallow 18 cm (7 inch) square tin which has been rinsed in cold water. Leave in a cool place to set.

When the mixture is firm, cut into 49 marshmallows.
Makes 49

Cider Turkish Delight

METRIC/IMPERIAL
300 ml/½ pint cider
25 g/1 oz gelatine
450 g/1 lb sugar
¼ teaspoon citric acid
2-3 drops vanilla
  essence
2-3 drops almond
  essence
To finish:
50 g/2 oz icing sugar
25 g/1 oz cornflour

AMERICAN
1¼ cups cider
4 envelopes
  unflavored gelatin
2 cups sugar
¼ teaspoon citric acid
2-3 drops vanilla
2-3 drops almond
  extract
To finish:
½ cup sifted
  confectioners'
  sugar
¼ cup cornstarch

Warm the cider in an 18 cm (7 inch) base diameter pan. Sprinkle the gelatine over the cider and stir until dissolved. Stir in the sugar and citric acid and heat gently until the sugar has completely dissolved. Bring to the boil and boil gently for 20 minutes, stirring occasionally.

Remove from the heat and leave to stand for 10 minutes – do not stir. Skim off the froth. Stir in the vanilla and almond essences (extracts). Pour into an 18 cm (7 inch) square tin (pan) and chill for 24 hours. Cut into 49 squares with a sharp, wet knife.

Sift together the icing (confectioners') sugar and cornflour (cornstarch) and toss the squares in the mixture. Place the Turkish Delight in paper sweet (candy) cases.
Makes 49

Chocolate Squares

METRIC/IMPERIAL
22 g (¾ oz) gelatine
4 tablespoons hot
  water
3 teaspoons cocoa
  powder
350 ml/12 fl oz
  evaporated milk
1¼ teaspoons liquid
  sweetener

AMERICAN
3 envelopes
  unflavored gelatin
¼ cup hot water
3 teaspoons
  sweetened cocoa
  powder
1½ cups evaporated
  milk
1¼ teaspoons liquid
  sweetener

Dissolve the gelatine in the hot water. Dissolve the cocoa in the milk in a bowl over a pan of hot water or in a double boiler. Bring to the boil and boil for 3 minutes.

Remove from the heat and stir in the gelatine and sweetener. Pour into an 18 cm (7 inch) square tin and chill until set. Cut into 25 squares.
Makes 25

Chocolate Coconut Ice

METRIC/IMPERIAL
1 × 225 g/8 oz can
  condensed milk
325 g/12 oz icing
  sugar, sieved
175 g/6 oz desiccated
  coconut
1 tablespoon cocoa
  powder

AMERICAN
1 × 8 oz can
  condensed milk
2⅔ cups sifted
  confectioners'
  sugar
2 cups shredded
  coconut
1 tablespoon
  unsweetened cocoa
  powder

Mix together all the ingredients in a bowl. Spoon the mixture into a greased 18 cm (7 inch) square tin (pan) and level the surface. Chill overnight. Cut into 36 squares.
Makes 36

Toffees, Boiled Sweets & Candies

To make the most of these sweets and candies, you will need a sugar thermometer to achieve perfect results, although you can follow the cold water tests (see page 5). Use a large, heavy-based pan and be careful as the mixtures do get very hot. Toffees need to be marked into pieces when still warm in the tin, then they can be easily broken into pieces when cold.

Cider Toffee Apples

METRIC/IMPERIAL	AMERICAN
6 small eating apples	6 small eating apples
225 g/8 oz soft dark brown sugar	1⅓ cups dark brown sugar
100 g/4 oz golden syrup	⅓ cup light corn syrup
6 tablespoons dry cider	6 tablespoons hard cider
25 g/1 oz butter	2 tablespoons butter
1 teaspoon vinegar	1 teaspoon vinegar

Wash and thoroughly dry the apples. Remove the stalks and push a wooden skewer or ice lolly (popsicle) stick into each apple.

Dissolve the sugar and syrup in the cider in a large, heavy-based pan over a gentle heat. Stir in the butter and vinegar. Bring to the boil and boil to the hard crack stage (150°C/300°F). Remove from the heat and quickly dip each apple in the toffee mixture, coating each one thoroughly. Dip the toffee apple immediately into cold water and stand on a greased baking tray to set.
Makes 6

Bonfire Toffee

METRIC/IMPERIAL	AMERICAN
450 g/1 lb demerara sugar	2⅔ cups brown sugar
150 ml/¼ pint water	⅔ cup water
75 g/3 oz butter, cut into cubes	¼ cup plus 2 tablespoons butter, cut into cubes
100 g/4 oz black treacle	⅓ cup molasses
100 g/4 oz golden syrup	⅓ cup light corn syrup
¼ teaspoon cream of tartar	¼ teaspoon cream of tartar
48 walnut halves	48 walnut halves

Place the sugar and water in a large, heavy-based pan and dissolve the sugar over a gentle heat. Stir in the butter, treacle (molasses), syrup and cream of tartar. Bring to the boil and boil to the soft crack stage (132°C/270°F). Remove from the heat and pour into a greased 10 × 30 cm (4 × 12 inch) tin (pan).

While the toffee is still warm, mark it into 48 squares and press a walnut half on each square. Leave in the tin until cold.
Makes 48

Bonfire Toffee; Cider Toffee Apples

Somerset Toffee

METRIC/IMPERIAL	AMERICAN
50 g/2 oz golden syrup	3 tablespoons light corn syrup
275 g/10 oz granulated sugar	1¼ cups sugar
50 g/2 oz butter	¼ cup butter
4 tablespoons cider	¼ cup cider
1 teaspoon vinegar	1 teaspoon vinegar
2 teaspoons bicarbonate of soda	2 teaspoons baking soda

Place the syrup, sugar, butter, cider and vinegar in a large, heavy-based pan. Bring to the boil and boil for 6 minutes. Remove from the heat and stir in the soda. Immediately pour into a greased 20 cm (8 inch) round tin (pan). Mark into diamonds while the toffee is still warm. Leave in the tin until cold.
Makes about 42

Honey and Lemon Toffee

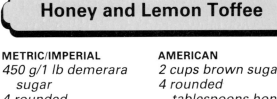

METRIC/IMPERIAL	AMERICAN
450 g/1 lb demerara sugar	2 cups brown sugar
4 rounded tablespoons clear honey	4 rounded tablespoons honey
175 g/6 oz butter	¾ cup butter
1 tablespoon lemon juice	1 tablespoon lemon juice

Place all the ingredients in a large pan and stir over a gentle heat until the sugar has dissolved. Bring the mixture to the boil, stirring only once or twice, and boil to the hard ball stage (118°C/245°F).

Pour the mixture into a greased 18 × 28 cm (7 × 11 inch) swiss roll tin (jelly roll pan) and leave to cool. Mark into 49 squares and break up when cold.
Makes 49

Barley Sugar Sticks

METRIC/IMPERIAL	AMERICAN
450 g/1 lb preserving sugar	2 cups preserving sugar
150 ml/¼ pint water	⅔ cup water
thinly pared rind and juice of 1 small lemon	thinly pared rind and juice of 1 small lemon
pinch of cream of tartar	pinch of cream of tartar

Dissolve the sugar in the water in a large, heavy-based pan over a gentle heat. Stir in the lemon rind and cream of tartar. Bring to the boil and boil to the soft ball stage (116°C/240°F). Remove from the heat. Lift out the lemon rind and stir in the lemon juice. Boil to the hard crack stage (154°C/310°F).

Pour the mixture on to a greased marble, enamel or wooden work surface and work the barley sugar from the outside to the centre with a greased, flexible palette knife until it is manageable. Form into a rope and pull. Snip into 10 cm (4 inch) strips with oiled scissors and bend over the ends.
Makes about 24
Illustrated on page 38

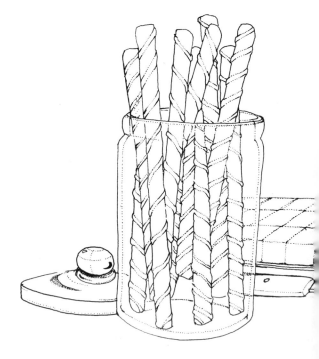

Barley Sugar Twists

METRIC/IMPERIAL	AMERICAN
225 g/8 oz preserving sugar	1 cup preserving sugar
150 ml/¼ pint water	⅔ cup water
225 g/8 oz powdered glucose	scant 2 cups powdered glucose
pinch of cream of tartar	pinch of cream of tartar
2-3 drops lemon essence	2-3 drops lemon extract

Dissolve the sugar in the water in a large, heavy-based pan over a gentle heat. Stir in the powdered glucose. Bring to the boil and boil to the hard crack stage (154°C/310°F). Stir in the cream of tartar and lemon essence (extract).

Pour on to a greased marble, enamel or wooden work surface. Work the barley sugar from the outside to the centre with a greased flexible palette knife until it is manageable. Twist and form into a rope and pull. Snip into 5 cm (2 inch) sticks with oiled scissors and twist.
Makes about 24

Caramels

METRIC/IMPERIAL	AMERICAN
75 g/3 oz margarine	¼ cup plus 2 tablespoons margarine
150 g/5 oz sugar	⅔ cup sugar
1 × 350 g/12 oz can sweetened condensed milk	1 × 12 oz can condensed milk
1 tablespoon golden syrup	1 tablespoon light corn syrup
2-3 drops vanilla essence	2-3 drops vanilla

Melt the margarine in a large, heavy-based pan over a gentle heat. Stir in the sugar, milk and syrup and stir until the sugar dissolves. Bring to the boil, stirring continuously and simmer for 20 minutes to the hard ball stage (130°C/265°F). Stir in the vanilla.

Pour the mixture into a greased 18 cm (7 inch) square tin (pan). Mark into 28 bars while still warm. Leave in the tin until cold.
Makes 28

Golden Toffee

METRIC/IMPERIAL	AMERICAN
100 g/4 oz butter	½ cup butter
225 g/8 oz granulated sugar	1 cup sugar
2 tablespoons vinegar	2 tablespoons vinegar
2 tablespoons golden syrup	2 tablespoons light corn syrup

Melt the butter in a large, heavy-based pan over a gentle heat. Add the sugar, vinegar and syrup and stir until the sugar has dissolved. Bring to the boil and boil until golden brown or at the hard ball stage (130°C/265°F).

Pour into a greased 18 cm (7 inch) square tin (pan). Mark into 28 bars while still warm. Leave in the tin until cold.
Makes 28

Nutty Toffee

METRIC/IMPERIAL	AMERICAN
225 g/8 oz butter	1 cup butter
450 g/1 lb demerara sugar	2⅔ cups brown sugar
2 tablespoons golden syrup	2 tablespoons light corn syrup
175 g/6 oz walnuts, chopped	1½ cups chopped walnuts

Cut the butter into pieces and place in a large, heavy-based pan with the sugar, syrup and nuts. Heat gently until the sugar has dissolved, stirring occasionally. Bring the mixture to the boil and boil rapidly for 4 to 5 minutes until thick, stirring constantly.

Spread the mixture immediately in a greased 28 × 20 cm (11 × 8 inch) Swiss roll tin (jelly roll pan). Leave for 5 minutes until just beginning to set, then cut into about 35 pieces and leave in the tin until cold.
Makes about 35

Honey and Nut Brittle

METRIC/IMPERIAL	AMERICAN
225 g/8 oz caster sugar	1 cup sugar
2 tablespoons clear honey	2 tablespoons honey
100 g/4 oz toasted almonds, chopped	1 cup toasted and chopped almonds

Place the sugar and honey in a heavy pan over a gentle heat until the sugar has dissolved, stirring once or twice. Bring to the boil and boil for 2 minutes. Stir in the nuts. Pour the mixture into a greased 18 cm (7 inch) square tin. Cut into 12 pieces while still warm. Leave in the tin until cold.
Makes 12

Cinnamon Cushions

METRIC/IMPERIAL	AMERICAN
450 g/1 lb soft brown sugar	2⅔ cups light brown sugar
50 g/2 oz butter	¼ cup butter
2 tablespoons golden syrup	2 tablespoons light corn syrup
150 ml/¼ pint water	⅔ cup water
½ teaspoon cream of tartar	½ teaspoon cream of tartar
½ teaspoon ground cinnamon	½ teaspoon ground cinnamon

Dissolve the sugar, butter and syrup in the water in a large, heavy-based pan over a gentle heat. Bring to the boil and add the cream of tartar. Boil to the soft crack stage (143°C/290°F) and stir in the cinnamon.

Pour the mixture on to a greased marble, enamel or wooden work surface and leave until a skin has formed. Work the toffee from the outside to the centre with a greased, flexible palette knife until manageable. Form into a rope and pull. Snip into 2.5 cm (1 inch) sticks with oiled scissors and press between finger and thumb to make cushion shapes.
Makes about 48
Illustrated on page 19

Nutty Toffee; Vanilla Fudge (page 37)

Chocolate Caramels

METRIC/IMPERIAL	AMERICAN
50 g/2 oz drinking chocolate powder	½ cup sweetened cocoa powder
175 g/6 oz golden syrup	½ cup light corn syrup
225 g/8 oz sugar	1 cup sugar
300 ml/½ pint single cream	1¼ cups light cream

Dissolve the drinking chocolate (sweetened cocoa), syrup and sugar in the cream in a fairly large, heavy-based pan over a gentle heat, stirring all the time. Bring to the boil slowly and cook gently for 1 hour, stirring occasionally to prevent sticking.

When the mixture is thick and reduced by half, pour into a greased 16 cm (6½ inch) square tin (pan) and chill. Mark into 36 pieces when still warm. Leave in the tin until cold. Wrap the caramel squares in waxed paper.
Makes 36

Honey and Treacle Toffee

METRIC/IMPERIAL	AMERICAN
4 tablespoons water	¼ cup water
100 g/4 oz butter	½ cup butter
450 g/1 lb soft brown sugar	3 cups soft brown sugar
2 tablespoons honey	2 tablespoons honey
1 tablespoon black treacle	1 tablespoon molasses

Place all the ingredients in a large, heavy-based pan and heat gently until the sugar has dissolved. Bring to the boil and boil to the hard crack stage (150°C/300°F).

Pour the toffee into a greased 15 cm (6 inch) square tin (pan) and leave to harden. Break into pieces with a small hammer.
Makes about 30

Almond Caramels

METRIC/IMPERIAL	AMERICAN
50 g/2 oz plain chocolate, grated	⅓ cup semisweet chocolate morsels
100 g/4 oz soft brown sugar	⅔ cup light brown sugar
150 ml/¼ pint milk	⅔ cup milk
350 g/12 oz golden syrup	1 cup light corn syrup
40 g/1½ oz butter	3 tablespoons butter
¼ teaspoon almond essence	¼ teaspoon almond extract
50 g/2 oz chopped almonds	½ cup chopped almonds

Place the chocolate, sugar, milk, syrup and butter in a heavy-based pan and bring slowly to the boil, stirring. Continue to boil gently to the hard ball stage (120°C/248°F).

Remove from the heat and stir in the almond essence (extract). Pour into a shallow greased 18 cm (7 inch) square tin (pan). Sprinkle over the chopped nuts. Mark into 2.5 cm (1 inch) squares and leave to set. When cold, cut into squares.
Makes 49

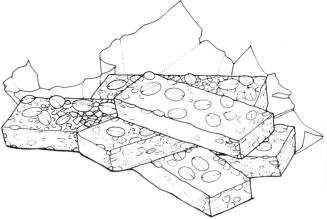

Nougat

METRIC/IMPERIAL	AMERICAN
3 egg whites	3 egg whites
2 tablespoons clear honey	2 tablespoons honey
350 g/12 oz sugar	1½ cups sugar
150 ml/¼ pint water	⅔ cup water
50 g/2 oz powdered glucose	½ cup powdered glucose
½ teaspoon vanilla essence	½ teaspoon vanilla
50 g/2 oz glacé cherries, chopped	¼ cup chopped glacé cherries
50 g/2 oz chopped mixed peel	⅓ cup chopped candied peel
150 g/5 oz unsalted almonds or peanuts, chopped	1¼ cups chopped unsalted almonds or peanuts

Dampen an 18 cm (7 inch) square tin (pan) and line it with rice paper.

Beat the egg whites in a deep bowl until stiff. Melt the honey in a bowl over a pan of hot water or in a double boiler. Beat the egg whites into the honey until smooth and pale. Remove from the heat.

Dissolve the sugar in the water in a pan over a low heat. Add the glucose and bring to the boil. Boil to the hard ball stage (130°C/265°F) without stirring. Pour the syrup over the honey mixture and add the vanilla. Whisk over hot water with an electric beater for about 25 minutes or to the hard ball stage (130°C/265°F). Stir in the cherries, peel and nuts. Pour into the prepared tin. Cover with rice paper and lay some weights or heavy cans on top. Chill then cut into 36 squares.
Makes 36

Fruit Caramels

METRIC/IMPERIAL	AMERICAN
50 g/2 oz stoned dates	⅓ cup pitted dates
50 g/2 oz dried figs	⅓ cup dried figs
75 g/3 oz seedless raisins	½ cup raisins
75 g/3 oz dried apricots	½ cup dried apricots
50 g/2 oz chopped mixed nuts	½ cup chopped mixed nuts
1 tablespoon lemon juice	1 tablespoon lemon juice
1 tablespoon clear honey	1 tablespoon honey
desiccated coconut to decorate	shredded coconut to decorate

Mince or very finely chop the dates, figs, raisins and apricots. Stir in the chopped nuts, lemon juice and honey. Press the mixture together in a bowl.

With damp hands, form the mixture into 20 balls and place in paper sweet (candy) cases. Sprinkle with the coconut.
Makes 20

Treacle Toffee

METRIC/IMPERIAL	AMERICAN
100 g/4 oz block margarine	½ cup block margarine
225 g/8 oz granulated sugar	1 cup sugar
3 tablespoons black treacle	3 tablespoons molasses
2 tablespoons vinegar	2 tablespoons vinegar

Melt the margarine in a large, heavy-based pan over a gentle heat. Add the sugar, treacle (molasses) and vinegar and stir until the sugar has dissolved. Bring to the boil and boil to the hard ball stage (130°C/265°F).

Pour into a greased 15 cm (6 inch) square tin (pan). Mark into 36 squares while still warm. Leave in the tin until cold.
Makes 36

All Kinds of Fudges

There's nothing quite as scrumptious as smooth and creamy homemade fudge. It is quick and easy to make and you can add chopped nuts, cherries, marshmallows or dates to ring the changes. Good homemade fudge should be soft in texture and simply melt in the mouth!

Chocolate Fudge

METRIC/IMPERIAL
200 g/7 oz plain chocolate, broken into pieces
25 g/1 oz butter, cut into cubes
1 egg, beaten
1 × 225 g/8 oz can condensed milk
450 g/1 lb icing sugar, sieved
½ teaspoon vanilla essence

AMERICAN
7 squares (1 oz each) semi-sweet chocolate
2 tablespoons butter, cut into cubes
1 egg, beaten
1 × 8 oz can condensed milk
3½ cups sifted confectioners' sugar
½ teaspoon vanilla

Melt the chocolate in a bowl over a pan of hot water or in a double boiler. Remove from the heat and beat in the butter and egg. Beat in the milk, sugar and vanilla and continue beating until the mixture thickens. Pour into a greased 18 cm (7 inch) square tin (pan), level the surface and mark into 36 squares. Chill the fudge and place in paper sweet (candy) cases when set.
Makes 36

Nutty Marshmallow Fudge

METRIC/IMPERIAL
225 g/8 oz sugar
100 g/4 oz plain flour
25 g/1 oz cocoa powder
100 g/4 oz butter
1 × 350 g/12 oz can condensed milk
75 g/3 oz walnuts, chopped
150 g/5 oz sweet biscuits, crushed
1 teaspoon vanilla essence
150 g/5 oz marshmallows

AMERICAN
1 cup sugar
1 cup all-purpose flour
¼ cup unsweetened cocoa powder
½ cup butter
1 × 12 oz can condensed milk
¾ cup chopped walnuts
1¾ cups graham cracker crumbs
1 teaspoon vanilla
5 oz marshmallows

Place the sugar, flour, cocoa, butter and condensed milk in a large, heavy-based pan and stir continuously over a gentle heat until the mixture comes to the boil; boil for 1 minute. Remove from the heat and leave to cool.

Stir in the walnuts, biscuit (cracker) crumbs and vanilla. Quickly stir in the marshmallows to give a marble effect. Pour the mixture into a greased 20 cm (8 inch) square tin (pan) and refrigerate. Cut into 36 squares when cold.
Makes 36

A selection of homemade fudge
(Photograph: Cadbury Typhoo Food Advisory Service)

Festival Fudge

METRIC/IMPERIAL	AMERICAN
250 ml/8 fl oz milk	1 cup miilk
450 g/1 lb caster sugar	2 cups sugar
4 tablespoons golden syrup	¼ cup light corn syrup
50 g/2 oz plain chocolate, broken into pieces	2 squares (1 oz each) semi-sweet chocolate, broken into pieces
2 teaspoons vanilla essence	2 teaspoons vanilla
1 teaspoon almond essence	1 teaspoon almond extract
225 g/8 oz glacé cherries, chopped	1 cup chopped glacé cherries
175 g/6 oz blanched almonds, toasted and chopped	1½ cups chopped and toasted almonds

Place the milk, sugar, syrup and chocolate in a large, heavy-based pan over a gentle heat and stir until the chocolate has melted and the sugar has dissolved. Bring to the boil and boil, without stirring, to the soft ball stage (114°C/238°F). Leave to cool for 30 minutes.

Beat in the vanilla and almond essences (extracts) until thick and smooth. Stir in the cherries and almonds. Pour into a greased 23 cm (9 inch) square tin (pan) and level the surface. Leave to set, then cut into 48 squares.
Makes 48
Illustrated on page 46

Speedy Chocolate Fudge

METRIC/IMPERIAL	AMERICAN
100 g/4 oz plain chocolate, broken into pieces	4 squares (1 oz each) semi-sweet chocolate, broken into pieces
50 g/2 oz butter	¼ cup butter
2 tablespoons milk	2 tablespoons milk
1 teaspoon vanilla essence	1 teaspoon vanilla
450 g/1 lb icing sugar, sieved	3½ cups sifted confectioners' sugar

Melt the chocolate and butter in a bowl over a pan of hot water or in a double boiler. Remove from the heat and stir in the milk and vanilla. Gradually beat in the icing (confectioners') sugar until smooth. Pour into a greased 18 cm (7 inch) square tin (pan) and level the surface with a knife. Refrigerate overnight and cut into 36 squares.
Makes 36

Milky Fudge

METRIC/IMPERIAL	AMERICAN
450 g/1 lb granulated sugar	2 cups sugar
4 rounded tablespoons honey	¼ cup honey
150 ml/¼ pint evaporated milk	⅔ cup evaporated milk
50 g/2 oz butter	¼ cup butter

Rinse out a large heavy-based pan with cold water. Place the sugar, honey and milk in the pan and melt over a gentle heat. Bring slowly to the boil and boil to the soft ball stage (114°C/238°F).

Add the butter but do not stir. Leave to cool a little. Beat with a wooden spoon until thick and creamy. Pour the fudge into a greased 18 cm (7 inch) square tin and leave until cold. Mark into 49 squares.
Makes 49

Chocolate and Cherry Fudge

METRIC/IMPERIAL	AMERICAN
50 g/2 oz butter	¼ cup butter
25 g/1 oz cocoa powder	¼ cup unsweetened cocoa powder
4 tablespoons water	4 tablespoons water
450 g/1 lb sugar	2 cups firmly packed sugar
1 × 200 g/7 oz can condensed milk	1 × 7 oz can condensed milk
100 g/4 oz glacé cherries, chopped	½ cup chopped glacé cherries

Place the butter, cocoa and water in a large, heavy-based pan and melt the butter over a gentle heat. Add the sugar and condensed milk and stir until the sugar has dissolved. Bring to the boil and boil gently to the soft ball stage (114°C/238°F).

Remove from the heat and beat really well until thick and smooth. Stir in the cherries. Pour into a greased 18 cm (7 inch) square tin (pan) and level the surface with a knife. Refrigerate overnight and cut into 36 squares.
Makes 36
Illustrated on page 19

Chocolate Mallow Fudge

METRIC/IMPERIAL	AMERICAN
350 g/12 oz caster sugar	1½ cups sugar
150 ml/¼ pint evaporated milk	⅔ cup evaporated milk
100 g/4 oz plain chocolate, broken into pieces	4 squares (1 oz each) semi-sweet chocolate
150 g/5 oz marshmallows	5 oz marshmallows
100 g/4 oz mixed nuts, chopped	1 cup chopped mixed nuts
2-3 drops vanilla essence	2-3 drops vanilla

Place the sugar, milk and chocolate in a large, heavy-based pan over a gentle heat and stir until the chocolate has melted and the sugar has dissolved. Bring to the boil and simmer gently for 3 minutes. Remove from the heat and stir in the marshmallows until almost melted. Stir in the nuts and vanilla. Pour into a greased 18 × 28 cm (7 × 11 inch) tin (pan) and refrigerate overnight. Cut the fudge into 40 pieces.
Makes 40

Chocolate Nut Fudge

METRIC/IMPERIAL	AMERICAN
50 g/2 oz butter	¼ cup butter
25 g/1 oz cocoa powder	¼ cup unsweetened cocoa powder
4 tablespoons water	¼ cup water
2 tablespoons honey	2 tablespoons honey
450 g/1 lb sugar	2 cups sugar
1 × 200 g/7 oz can condensed milk	1 × 7 oz can condensed milk
50 g/2 oz walnuts, chopped	½ cup chopped walnuts

Place the butter, cocoa and water in a large, heavy-based pan and melt the butter over a gentle heat. Add the honey, sugar and condensed milk and stir until the sugar has dissolved. Bring to the boil and boil gently to the soft ball stage (114°C/238°F). Remove from the heat and cool slightly.

Beat the fudge mixture really well until thick and smooth. Stir in the walnuts. Pour into a greased 18 cm (7 inch) square tin (pan) and level the surface with a knife. Refrigerate overnight and cut into 36 pieces.

Makes 36

Note: Instead of the chopped walnuts, you can use chopped almonds or chopped unsalted peanuts in this recipe.

Crackle Fudge Squares

METRIC/IMPERIAL	AMERICAN
Base:	**Base:**
50 g/2 oz butter	¼ cup butter
50 g/2 oz toffees	2 oz caramels
50 g/2 oz rice cereal	2 cups rice cereal
Topping:	**Topping:**
50 g/2 oz butter	¼ cup butter
4 tablespoons water	¼ cup water
2 tablespoons golden syrup	2 tablespoons light corn syrup
450 g/1 lb sugar	2 cups sugar
120 ml/4 fl oz sweetened condensed milk	½ cup sweetened condensed milk

To make the base: melt the butter and toffees in a pan over a gentle heat, stirring all the time. Stir in the rice cereal until thoroughly coated. Spoon the mixture into a well greased 15 cm (6 inch) square tin (pan) and press down well. Chill.

Place the butter, water, syrup, sugar and milk in a deep, heavy-based pan over a moderate heat. Stir until the sugar has dissolved, then bring to the boil. Boil gently for 10 minutes without stirring.

Remove from the heat and beat well for 5 minutes. Pour on to the chilled base and leave until cold. Cut into 36 squares.

Makes 36

Chocolate Nut Fudge
(Photograph: Cadbury Typhoo Food Advisory Service)

Marshmallow Fudge

METRIC/IMPERIAL	AMERICAN
150 g/5 oz marshmallows	5 oz marshmallows
2 tablespoons milk	2 tablespoons milk
50 g/2 oz caster sugar	¼ cup sugar
50 g/2 oz butter	¼ cup butter
100 g/4 oz icing sugar, sieved	1 scant cup sifted confectioners' sugar
50 g/2 oz glacé cherries, chopped	¼ cup chopped glacé cherries
50 g/2 oz almonds, roasted and chopped	½ cup roasted and chopped almonds

Melt the marshmallows with 1 tablespoon of the milk in a pan over a gentle heat.

Heat the remaining milk, caster sugar and butter in another pan and stir until the sugar has dissolved. Bring to the boil and boil briskly for 5 minutes. Remove from the heat. Stir in the melted marshmallows and icing (confectioners') sugar, cherries and almonds. Spoon into a greased 15 cm (6 inch) square tin (pan) and level the surface. Chill in the refrigerator, then cut into 24 squares.
Makes 24

Honey and Date Fudge

METRIC/IMPERIAL	AMERICAN
100 g/4 oz honey	⅓ cup honey
450 g/1 lb caster sugar	2 cups sugar
150 ml/¼ pint water	⅔ cup water
¼ teaspoon cream of tartar	¼ teaspoon cream of tartar
2 egg whites	2 egg whites
50 g/2 oz stoned dates, chopped	⅓ cup pitted and chopped dates

Place the honey, sugar, water and cream of tartar in a large, heavy-based pan and heat gently until the sugar has dissolved. Bring to the boil and boil to the hard ball stage (130°C/265°F). Remove from the heat.

Whisk the egg whites until stiff and pour on the boiling syrup, whisking it vigorously until thick. Stir in the dates. Pour into a greased 10 × 30 cm (4 × 12 inch) tin (pan) and chill until set. Cut into 24 squares with a hot, wet knife.
Makes 24

Melt-in-the-Mouth Fudge

METRIC/IMPERIAL	AMERICAN
450 g/1 lb sugar	2 cups sugar
50 g/2 oz butter	¼ cup butter
150 ml/¼ pint evaporated milk	⅔ cup evaporated milk
150 ml/¼ pint milk	⅔ cup milk
2-3 drops vanilla essence	2-3 drops vanilla

Place the sugar, butter and milks in a large, heavy-based pan and stir over a gentle heat until the sugar has dissolved. Bring to the boil and boil to soft ball stage (114°C/238°F), stirring occasionally. Remove from the heat.

Beat in the vanilla and continue beating until the mixture is thick and creamy. Pour into a greased 15 cm (6 inch) square tin (pan). Mark into 24 squares while still warm. Leave in the tin until cold.
Makes 24
Illustrated on page 38

Fruit and Nut Fudge

METRIC/IMPERIAL	AMERICAN
2 tablespoons water	2 tablespoons water
50 g/2 oz butter	¼ cup butter
450 g/1 lb granulated sugar	2 cups sugar
300 ml/½ pint evaporated milk	1¼ cups evaporated milk
½ teaspoon vanilla essence	½ teaspoon vanilla
100 g/4 oz dried mixed fruit	⅔ cup dried mixed fruit
50 g/2 oz chopped nuts	½ cup chopped nuts

Put the water and butter in heavy-based pan and heat until the butter has melted. Add the sugar and milk and stir over a low heat until the sugar has dissolved. Add the vanilla essence. Bring the mixture to the boil and add the fruit and nuts. Boil the mixture, stirring frequently, to the soft ball stage (113°C/235°F).

Beat the mixture until cloudy, then pour into a well greased 18 cm (7 inch) square tin. Allow to set then cut into 36 pieces with a sharp knife.
Makes 36

Vanilla Fudge

METRIC/IMPERIAL
2 tablespoons golden
  syrup
3 tablespoons water
75 g/3 oz butter
450 g/1 lb caster
  sugar
1 × 175 g/6 oz can
  sweetened
  condensed milk
2-3 drops vanilla
  essence

AMERICAN
2 tablespoons light
  corn syrup
3 tablespoons water
¼ cup plus
  2 tablespoons
  butter
2 cups sugar
1 × 6 oz can
  condensed milk
2-3 drops vanilla

Place the syrup, water, butter, sugar and condensed milk in a large, heavy-based pan and stir over a gentle heat until the sugar has dissolved. Bring to the boil and boil to soft ball stage (116°C/240°F). Remove from the heat.

Beat in the vanilla and continue beating until thick and creamy. Pour into a greased 18 cm (7 inch) square tin (pan). Mark into 36 squares while still warm. Leave the fudge in the tin until cold.
Makes 36
Illustrated on page 27

Milk Chocolate Fudge

METRIC/IMPERIAL
1 teaspoon gelatine
450 g/1 lb caster
  sugar
300 ml/½ pint milk
3 tablespoons
  drinking chocolate
  powder
50 g/2 oz butter
½ teaspoon vanilla
  essence
pinch of cream of
  tartar
pinch of salt
glacé cherries and
  walnut halves to
  decorate

AMERICAN
1 teaspoon
  unflavored gelatin
2 cups sugar
1¼ cups milk
3 tablespoons
  sweetened cocoa
  powder
¼ cup butter
½ teaspoon vanilla
pinch of cream of
  tartar
pinch of salt
glacé cherries and
  walnut halves to
  decorate

Place all the ingredients in an 18 cm (7 inch) base diameter pan. Stir over a gentle heat until the sugar has dissolved. Boil gently, without stirring, for about 30 minutes to the soft ball stage (114°C/238°F).

Leave the mixture until it is cool enough for the pan to be held on the palm of the hand, then whisk until very thick and creamy. Pour into a greased 18 cm (7 inch) square tin (pan). Mark into 36 squares while still warm. Decorate with cherries and walnuts then chill.

Remove from the tin and place in paper sweet (candy) cases.
Makes 36
Illustrated on page 14

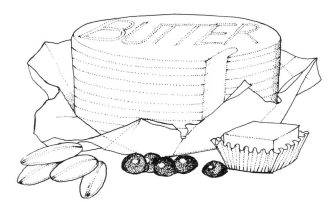

Fondants & Creams

Many of these uncooked sweets and candies are simple enough for children to make – they'll have fun and enjoy the delicious end result as well! Soft and creamy, these candies can be coloured and flavoured in various ways and cut into pretty shapes with tiny cutters. Uncooked fondant tends to harden so eat these up quickly.

Fondant Fancies

METRIC/IMPERIAL	AMERICAN
450 g/1 lb sugar	2 cups sugar
150 ml/¼ pint water	⅔ cup water
¼ teaspoon cream of tartar	¼ teaspoon cream of tartar
selection of food colourings and flavourings	selection of food colorings and flavorings

Dissolve the sugar in the water in a large, heavy-based pan over a gentle heat. Bring to the boil and stir in the cream of tartar. Boil to the soft ball stage (116°C/240°F). To prevent crystals forming, brush down the sides of the pan with a damp brush.

Sprinkle some cold water in a wide heatproof bowl. Pour in the syrup and leave for 15 minutes until a skin forms over the surface. Work the mixture quickly with a metal palette knife in a figure of eight until the fondant is white and manageable. Knead until smooth.

Divide the fondant and colour and flavour as required. Stand the fondant you are not using in a bowl over a pan of hot water or in a double boiler to keep it soft. Roll out the fondant on a dry work surface, lightly sprinkled with sieved icing (confectioners') sugar, and cut out with fancy cutters. Leave to dry then place in paper sweet (candy) cases.

Barley Sugar Sticks (page 24); Melt-in-the-Mouth Fudge (page 36); Fondant Fancies; Coconut Ice (page 18)
(Photograph: British Sugar Bureau)

Valentines

METRIC/IMPERIAL	AMERICAN
450 g/1 lb icing sugar, sieved	3½ cups sifted confectioners' sugar
50 g/2 oz liquid glucose	2 oz liquid glucose
1 egg white, whisked	1 egg white, whisked
3 teaspoons lemon juice	3 teaspoons lemon juice
red food colouring	red food coloring
raspberry flavouring	raspberry flavoring

Mix together all the ingredients in a bowl to form a stiff paste and knead until smooth. Roll out on a work surface liberally dusted with icing (confectioners') sugar. Cut out the Valentines using a heart-shaped cutter and leave them to dry.

Orange Creams

METRIC/IMPERIAL	AMERICAN
40 g/1½ oz full fat soft cheese	¼ cup full fat soft cheese
finely grated rind of 1 orange	finely grated rind of 1 orange
200 g/7 oz icing sugar, sieved	1½ cups sifted confectioners' sugar

Cream the cheese and orange rind together. Work in the icing (confectioners') sugar until the mixture is manageable.

Roll out on a work surface liberally sprinkled with icing (confectioners') sugar. Using assorted cutters, cut out different shaped sweets (candies). Leave them overnight on non-stick (parchment) paper to dry.

Next day arrange in paper sweet (candy) cases.

Makes about 14

Chocolate Peppermint Roll

METRIC/IMPERIAL	AMERICAN
450 g/1 lb icing sugar	2¾ cups confectioners' sugar
3 teaspoons gelatine	3 teaspoons gelatin
4 tablespoons hot water	¼ cup hot water
1 tablespoon glycerine	1 tablespoon glycerine
green food colouring	green food coloring
peppermint essence	peppermint extract
2 tablespoons cornflour	2 tablespoons cornstarch
50 g/2 oz plain chocolate	2 squares (1 oz each) chocolate

Sift the icing (confectioners') sugar into a bowl and make a well in the centre.

Add the gelatine to the hot water and stir briskly with a fork until dissolved. Add the gelatine to the sugar with the glycerine. Using a fork and working from the centre, gradually incorporate the sugar. Add a few drops of colouring and peppermint essence (extract) to taste and mix well.

Turn the mixture on to a board coated with cornflour (cornstarch). Knead lightly and roll into a ball. Cover with cling film (plastic wrap) to prevent drying out and leave for 24 hours.

Turn the mixture on to a board again coated with cornflour (cornstarch). Roll into 2.5 cm/1 inch wide rolls and then slice into small pieces.

Melt the chocolate in a heatproof bowl over a pan of hot water; leave to cool slightly. Dip the peppermints in the chocolate and lay on non-stick (parchment) paper. Chill until firm.

Coffee Walnut Creams

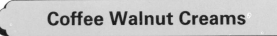

METRIC/IMPERIAL	AMERICAN
40 g/1½ oz full fat soft cheese	¼ cup full fat soft cheese
2 teaspoons strong black coffee	2 teaspoons strong black coffee
225 g/8 oz icing sugar, sieved	1¾ cups sifted confectioners' sugar
50 g/2 oz plain chocolate, broken into pieces	2 squares (1 oz each) semi-sweet chocolate, broken into pieces
16 walnut halves	16 walnut halves

Cream the cheese and coffee together. Work in the icing (confectioners') sugar until the mixture is manageable.

Roll into 16 balls on a work surface liberally sprinkled with icing (confectioners') sugar. Arrange the sweets (candies) on non-stick (parchment) paper, press them flat and leave to dry overnight.

Melt the chocolate in a bowl over a pan of hot water or in a double boiler. Remove from the heat. Place a blob of chocolate on each sweet (candy) and press on a walnut half. Leave to set.

Makes 16

Illustrated on page 51

Peppermint Mice

METRIC/IMPERIAL	AMERICAN
450 g/1 lb icing sugar, sieved	3½ cups sifted confectioners' sugar
3 tablespoons liquid glucose	3 tablespoons liquid glucose
1 egg white, lightly whisked	1 egg white, lightly whisked
few drops of peppermint essence	few drops of peppermint extract
Decoration:	**Decoration:**
24 currants	24 currants
12 coloured balls	12 colored balls
24 pieces angelica	24 pieces angelica
24 flaked almonds	24 slivered almonds
12 pieces string	12 pieces string

Place the sugar and glucose in a bowl. Add enough of the egg white to make a manageable mixture. Knead in the peppermint to taste.

Divide the mixture into 12 pieces and shape into "mice" on a liberally sugared surface. Decorate the mice using the currants for eyes, the coloured balls for noses, the angelica for whiskers, the almonds for ears and the string for tails.
Makes 12

Peanut Butter Creams

METRIC/IMPERIAL	AMERICAN
40 g/1½ oz full fat soft cheese	¼ cup full fat soft cheese
200 g/7 oz icing sugar, sieved	1½ cups sifted confectioners' sugar
2 tablespoons peanut butter	2 tablespoons peanut butter
2-3 drops vanilla essence	2-3 drops vanilla
25 g/1 oz salted peanuts, finely chopped	¼ cup finely chopped salted peanuts

Cream the cheese with the sugar, peanut butter and vanilla. Add more sugar if needed to give a manageable paste.

Roll the mixture into 10 balls and roll each one in the chopped peanuts to coat completely. Place in paper sweet (candy) cases.
Makes 10

Chocolate Treats

METRIC/IMPERIAL	AMERICAN
75 g/3 oz plain chocolate, broken into pieces	3 squares (1 oz each) semi-sweet chocolate, broken into pieces
50 g/2 oz butter	¼ cup butter
2 tablespoons golden syrup	2 tablespoons light corn syrup
2 tablespoons dried milk powder	2 tablespoons dried milk powder
14 chocolate buttons	14 chocolate buttons

Melt the chocolate pieces in a bowl over a pan of hot water or in a double boiler. Using a teaspoon, spoon the chocolate into 14 foil sweet (candy) cases to line them. Chill until set.

Melt the butter and syrup in a pan over a gentle heat. Stir in the dried milk powder. Bring to the boil and cook until golden brown in colour. Remove from the heat and leave to cool. Pour into the chocolate cases. When the filling begins to set, top each sweet (candy) with a chocolate button.
Makes 14

Rosehip Dreams

METRIC/IMPERIAL	AMERICAN
225 g/8 oz icing sugar, sieved	1¾ cups sifted confectioners' sugar
1 tablespoon rosehip syrup	1 tablespoon rosehip syrup
1 tablespoon lemon juice	1 tablespoon lemon juice
finely grated rind of ½ lemon	finely grated rind of ½ lemon
20 crystallized flowers to decorate	20 crystallized flowers to decorate

Mix the icing (confectioners') sugar, rosehip syrup, lemon juice and rind to a stiff paste. Roll into 20 balls on a work surface liberally sprinkled with icing (confectioners') sugar.

Press a crystallized flower on each and place in paper sweet (candy) cases. Chill.
Makes 20

Apricot Creams

METRIC/IMPERIAL	AMERICAN
50 g/2 oz unsalted butter	¼ cup unsalted butter
4 tablespoons water	¼ cup water
225 g/8 oz soft brown sugar	1¼ cups light brown sugar
1 teaspoon lemon juice	1 teaspoon lemon juice
4 tablespoons single cream	¼ cup light cream
175 g/6 oz dried apricots, chopped	1 cup chopped dried apricots
2 tablespoons soft brown sugar to decorate	2 tablespoons light brown sugar to decorate

Melt the butter in a deep pan, add the water, sugar and lemon juice. Bring the mixture to the boil and stir continuously until the mixture reaches 115°C/240°F on a sugar thermometer. Remove from the heat and add the cream. Return to the heat and stir continuously until the mixture reaches 150°C/300°F.

Remove from the heat and stir in the chopped apricots. Leave the mixture until cold. Form into 26 balls and roll in the sugar. Place in paper sweet (candy) cases.
Makes 26

Peppermint Creams

METRIC/IMPERIAL	AMERICAN
450 g/1 lb icing sugar, sieved	3½ cups sifted confectioners' sugar
few drops of peppermint essence	few drops of peppermint extract
1 egg white, lightly whisked	1 egg white, lightly whisked
few drops of green food colouring	few drops of green food coloring
25 g/1 oz chocolate	1 square (1 oz) semi-sweet chocolate

Mix the icing (confectioners') sugar and peppermint with enough egg white to make a stiff paste. Divide the mixture in half and colour one portion green.

Roll each portion into 18 balls on a work surface liberally sprinkled with icing (confectioners') sugar. Flatten each sweet (candy) with a fork.

Melt the chocolate in a bowl over a pan of hot water or in a double boiler. Half dip some of the peppermint creams in the chocolate. Leave all the peppermint creams overnight on non-stick (parchment) paper to dry.

Next day arrange the peppermint creams in paper sweet (candy) cases.
Makes 36

Fruity Clusters (page 61); Fudge; Coconut Ice; Peppermint Creams; and assorted truffles (Photograph: British Sugar Bureau)

Velvet Rolls

METRIC/IMPERIAL
150 ml/¼ pint
  evaporated milk
275 g/10 oz caster
  sugar
150 g/5 oz plain
  chocolate, broken
  into pieces
25 g/1 oz butter
finely grated rind of
  1 orange
225 g/8 oz icing sugar,
  sieved

AMERICAN
⅔ cup evaporated
  milk
1¼ cups sugar
5 squares (1 oz each)
  semi-sweet
  chocolate, broken
  into pieces
2 tablespoons butter
finely grated rind of
  1 orange
2 scant cups sifted
  confectioners'
  sugar

Reserve 1 tablespoon of the evaporated milk and pour the rest into a pan. Add the sugar and stir over a gentle heat until the sugar has dissolved. Bring to the boil and boil gently for 3 minutes. Stir in the chocolate until melted. Cool the mixture, beating occasionally.

Pour the mixture on to non-stick (parchment) paper making two 10 × 25 cm (4 × 10 inch) rectangles.

Cream the butter with the orange rind and gradually beat in the icing (confectioners') sugar and reserved evaporated milk. Knead until smooth. Divide the mixture in half and form into two 25 cm (10 inch) rolls. Put these on the chocolate rectangles and roll up in the paper. Chill until firm. Slice the rolls into 48 thin slices and place in paper sweet (candy) cases.
Makes 48
Illustrated on page 46

Santa's Treats

METRIC/IMPERIAL
25 g/1 oz butter
2 tablespoons cocoa
  powder, sieved
150 ml/¼ pint
  sweetened
  condensed milk
225 g/8 oz digestive
  biscuits, crushed
50 g/2 oz glacé
  cherries, chopped
50 g/2 oz hazelnuts,
  roasted and
  chopped
finely grated rind and
  juice of 1 orange
50 g/2 oz desiccated
  coconut

AMERICAN
2 tablespoons butter
2 tablespoons sifted
  unsweetened cocoa
  powder
⅔ cup sweetened
  condensed milk
2 cups graham
  cracker crumbs
¼ cup chopped glacé
  cherries
½ cup roasted and
  chopped hazelnuts
finely grated rind and
  juice of 1 orange
⅔ cup shredded
  coconut

Place the butter, cocoa and milk in a pan and melt together over a gentle heat. Remove from the heat and stir in the biscuit (cracker) crumbs, cherries, nuts and orange rind and juice.

With damp hands, shape the mixture into 36 balls and roll in the coconut. Place the sweets (candies) in paper sweet (candy) cases.
Makes 36

Chocolate Thimbles

METRIC/IMPERIAL	AMERICAN
150 g/5 oz plain chocolate, broken into pieces	5 squares (1 oz each) semi-sweet chocolate, broken into pieces
2 tablespoons strong coffee	2 tablespoons strong coffee
25 g/1 oz butter	2 tablespoons butter
1 egg yolk	1 egg yolk
toasted hazelnuts to decorate	toasted hazelnuts to decorate

Melt half the chocolate in a bowl over a pan of hot water or in a double boiler. Using a teaspoon, spoon some of the melted chocolate into 10 paper sweet (candy) cases. Tilt the cases to allow the chocolate to completely coat the inside of the cases. Repeat to give a good coating. Chill until set.

When firm, peel the paper cases from the chocolate to give 10 chocolate shells.

Melt the rest of the chocolate in a bowl over a pan of hot water or in a double boiler. Remove from the heat, beat well and beat in the coffee, butter and egg yolk. Chill the mixture.

When the filling is almost set, spoon into a piping (pastry) bag fitted with a small star nozzle. Pipe the mixture into the chocolate cases and decorate with toasted hazelnuts.
Makes 10

Peppermint Squares

METRIC/IMPERIAL	AMERICAN
175 g/6 oz butter	¾ cup butter
175 g/6 oz soft brown sugar	1 cup light brown sugar
2 eggs	2 eggs
150 g/5 oz self-raising flour, sieved	1¼ cups sifted all-purpose flour
25 g/1 oz cocoa powder, sieved	¼ cup unsweetened cocoa powder
Topping:	**Topping:**
2 tablespoons peppermint cordial	2 tablespoons peppermint cordial
100 g/4 oz sugar	½ cup sugar
2 tablespoons water	2 tablespoons water

Cream together the butter and brown sugar until pale and fluffy. Beat in the eggs. Fold in the flour and cocoa. Spoon into a greased 33 × 23 cm (13 × 9 inch) Swiss roll tin (jelly roll pan) and level the surface with a knife. Cook in a preheated moderate oven (180°C/350°F, Gas Mark 4) for 30 to 40 minutes.

To make the topping: mix the peppermint cordial with the sugar and water. Spread the paste over the cooked mixture as soon as it comes out of the oven. Leave in the tin until cold. Cut into 48 squares.
Makes 48

Assorted Fondants

METRIC/IMPERIAL	AMERICAN
2 egg whites	2 egg whites
450 g/1 lb icing sugar, sieved	3½ cups confectioners' sugar
yellow food colouring	yellow food coloring
lemon juice	lemon juice
red food colouring	red food coloring
raspberry flavouring	raspberry flavoring
almond essence	almond extract

Whisk the egg whites lightly and gradually beat in the sugar. Divide the fondant mixture into three separate bowls. Add a few drops of yellow food colouring and a few drops of lemon juice to one portion and mix it in. Add a few drops of red colouring to make another portion pale pink and add raspberry flavouring to taste. To the third portion, simply add a few drops of almond essence (extract).

Roll out each portion separately and cut into pretty shapes with fancy cutters. Leave the fondants to dry out and harden before storing.

Chocolate Sweets & Candies

Chocolate has been called the world's favourite flavour and it is certainly popular with everyone. It can be used to make all sorts of tempting truffles and other goodies. Take care when melting chocolate that you do not overheat it and remember to store chocolate sweets and candies in a cool place.

Chocolate Almond Truffles

METRIC/IMPERIAL
150 g/5 oz plain chocolate, broken into pieces
150 ml/¼ pint evaporated milk
2 teaspoons brandy
50 g/2 oz ground almonds
50 g/2 oz toasted almonds, chopped

AMERICAN
5 squares (1 oz each) semi-sweet chocolate, broken into pieces
⅔ cup evaporated milk
2 teaspoons brandy
½ cup ground almonds
½ cup toasted and chopped almonds

Melt the chocolate and evaporated milk in a bowl over a pan of hot water or in a double boiler. Continue cooking over a gentle heat for 15 minutes. Remove from the heat and cool, beating occasionally. Stir in the brandy and ground almonds. Chill the mixture.

Liberally sprinkle some icing (confectioners') sugar on the work surface and roll the mixture into 16 balls. Toss in the toasted almonds and place in paper sweet (candy) cases.
Makes 16

Muesli Squares

METRIC/IMPERIAL
150 g/5 oz plain chocolate, broken into pieces
3 tablespoons golden syrup
25 g/1 oz butter
225 g/8 oz muesli
150 g/5 oz milk chocolate, broken into pieces

AMERICAN
5 squares (1 oz each) semi-sweet chocolate, broken into pieces
3 tablespoons light corn syrup
2 tablespoons butter
½ lb granola
5 squares (1 oz each) milk chocolate, broken into pieces

Melt the plain (semi-sweet) chocolate, syrup and butter in a bowl over a pan of hot water or in a double boiler. Remove from the heat and stir in the muesli (granola). Press the mixture into a greased 18 cm (7 inch) square tin (pan) and chill.

Melt the milk chocolate in a bowl over a pan of hot water or in a double boiler and spread over the cereal mixture. Decorate the top with a fork and chill. Cut into 36 squares.
Makes 36

Chocolate Almond Truffles; Velvet Rolls (page 44); Marshmallows; Festival Fudge (page 32); Almond Candies (page 8)

Rum Truffles

METRIC/IMPERIAL
100 g/4 oz plain
    chocolate, broken
    into pieces
50 g/2 oz butter
100 g/4 oz icing sugar,
    sieved
100 g/4 oz cake
    crumbs
1 egg yolk
2 tablespoons rum
chopped nuts to
    decorate

AMERICAN
4 squares (1 oz each)
    semi-sweet
    chocolate, broken
    into pieces
¼ cup butter
1 cup sifted
    confectioners'
    sugar
2 cups cake crumbs
1 egg yolk
2 tablespoons rum
chopped nuts to
    decorate

Melt the chocolate and butter in a deep bowl over a pan of hot water or in a double boiler. Remove from the heat. Stir in the sugar, cake crumbs and egg yolk. Add the rum to taste. Spoon the mixture on to a plate and leave in a cold place until firm.

With damp hands, roll the mixture into 20 balls and roll them in the nuts. Place in paper sweet (candy) cases and chill.
Makes 20

Chocolate Nut Drops

METRIC/IMPERIAL
225 g/8 oz plain
    chocolate, broken
    into pieces
25 g/1 oz almonds,
    chopped
25 g/1 oz raisins
25 g/1 oz glacé
    cherries, chopped
2 tablespoons instant
    coffee granules

AMERICAN
8 squares (1 oz each)
    semi-sweet
    chocolate, broken
    into pieces
¼ cup chopped
    almonds
3 tablespoons raisins
3 tablespoons
    chopped glacé
    cherries
2 tablespoons instant
    coffee granules

Melt the chocolate in a bowl over a pan of hot water or in a double boiler. Remove from the heat. Stir in the almonds, raisins and cherries. Fold through the coffee.

Place 22 teaspoons of the mixture on non-stick (parchment) paper and press each one into a circle. Chill until firm.
Makes 22

Chocolate and Walnut Surprise

METRIC/IMPERIAL
100 g/4 oz plain
    cooking chocolate,
    broken into pieces
15 walnut pieces
4 tablespoons cider
100 g/4 oz plain
    chocolate, broken
    into pieces
175 g/6 oz icing sugar,
    sieved

AMERICAN
4 squares (1 oz each),
    cooking chocolate,
    broken into pieces
15 walnut pieces
¼ cup cider
4 squares (1 oz each)
    semi-sweet
    chocolate, broken
    into pieces
1⅓ cups sifted
    confectioners'
    sugar

Melt the cooking chocolate in a bowl over a pan of hot water or in a double boiler. Remove from the heat. Using a teaspoon, coat the inside of 15 paper sweet (candy) cases with the melted chocolate. Coat twice if liked, and chill until set.

Carefully peel the paper cases from the chocolate cups and place each cup into a clean paper sweet (candy) case. Put a piece of walnut in each cup.

Pour the cider into a small pan and boil rapidly until reduced by half; leave to cool. Melt the chocolate in a bowl over a pan of hot water or in a double boiler. Remove from the heat. Beat in the icing (confectioners') sugar and reduced cider. Add a drop of water if the mixture seems too stiff to pipe. Spoon the mixture into a piping (pastry) bag and pipe it into the chocolate cases. Chill.
Makes 15

Trifle Truffles

METRIC/IMPERIAL
15 g/½ oz glacé
   cherries, chopped
15 g/½ oz chopped
   mixed peel
1 tablespoon sherry
150 g/5 oz chocolate,
   broken into pieces
2 individual trifle
   sponge cakes
25 g/1 oz ground
   almonds
silver balls to
   decorate

AMERICAN
1½ tablespoons
   chopped glacé
   cherries
1½ tablespoons
   chopped mixed
   peel
1 tablespoon sherry
5 squares (1 oz each)
   chocolate, broken
   into pieces
2 individual dessert
   sponge shells
¼ cup ground
   almonds
silver balls to
   decorate

Soak the chopped cherries and peel in the sherry for 15 minutes. Melt the chocolate in a bowl over a pan of hot water or in a double boiler.

Crumble the sponges into the cherry mixture and stir in 2 tablespoons melted chocolate and the almonds. Make rough heaps of the mixture on a sheet of foil and chill.

Melt the remaining chocolate again and use it to carefully coat the truffles. Decorate with silver balls.
Makes about 15

Chocolate Orange Truffles

METRIC/IMPERIAL
100 g/4 oz cake
   crumbs
25 g/1 oz drinking
   chocolate powder
50 g/2 oz caster sugar
50 g/2 oz ground
   almonds
1-2 tablespoons
   orange juice
65 g/2½ oz butter,
   melted
extra drinking
   chocolate powder
   to decorate

AMERICAN
2 cups cake crumbs
¼ cup sweetened
   cocoa powder
¼ cup sugar
½ cup ground
   almonds
1-2 tablespoons
   orange juice
¼ cup plus 1
   tablespoon melted
   butter
extra sweetened
   cocoa powder to
   decorate

Place the cake crumbs, chocolate (cocoa) powder, sugar, ground almonds and orange juice in a bowl. Stir in enough of the melted butter to form a stiff paste.

Roll the mixture into 20 balls and coat the truffles in some drinking chocolate (cocoa) powder. Place in paper sweet (candy) cases.
Makes 20

Chocolate Truffles

METRIC/IMPERIAL
75 g/3 oz full fat soft
  cheese
1 teaspoon milk
100 g/4 oz icing sugar,
  sieved
100 g/4 oz drinking
  chocolate powder
chocolate vermicelli
  to decorate

AMERICAN
⅓ cup full fat soft
  cheese
1 teaspoon milk
1 scant cup sifted
  confectioners'
  sugar
1 cup sweetened
  cocoa powder
chocolate sprinkles to
  decorate

Cream together the cheese and milk. Gradually work in the icing (confectioners') sugar and chocolate (cocoa) powder to give a stiff mixture.

Shape the mixture into 20 balls and coat with the chocolate vermicelli (sprinkles). Place in paper sweet (candy) cases and chill.
Makes 20

Chocolate Lemon Bars

METRIC/IMPERIAL
3 tablespoons lemon
  curd
75 g/3 oz Ricicles
175 g/6 oz plain
  chocolate

AMERICAN
3 tablespoon lemon
  cheese
3 cups rice cereal
6 squares (1 oz each)
  semisweet
  chocolate

Place lemon curd into a small pan and bring to the boil, stirring. Boil for 1 minute, allow to cool slightly, and then stir in the rice cereal.

Spoon the mixture into a greased 18 cm/ 7 inch square tin and press down well.

Melt the chocolate in a heatproof bowl over a pan of hot water and spread over the mixture in the tin. Leave to set then cut into 15 fingers.
Makes 15

Florentines

METRIC/IMPERIAL
50 g/2 oz soft
  margarine
50 g/2 oz caster sugar
50 g/2 oz chopped
  mixed nuts
1½ tablespoons
  chopped raisins
1½ tablespoons
  chopped glacé
  cherries
1½ tablespoons
  chopped mixed
  peel
1 tablespoon plain
  flour
50 g/2 oz cooking
  chocolate

AMERICAN
¼ cup soft margarine
¼ cup sugar
½ cup chopped
  mixed nuts
1½ tablespoons
  chopped raisins
1½ tablespoons
  chopped glacé
  cherries
1½ tablespoons
  chopped mixed
  peel
1 tablespoon
  all-purpose flour
2 squares (1 oz each)
  cooking chocolate

Line two baking sheets with non-stick (parchment) paper. Melt the margarine in a pan over a gentle heat. Add the sugar and allow it to dissolve, then boil for 1 minute. Remove from the heat and stir in the nuts, raisins, cherries, peel and flour and mix thoroughly.

Drop small teaspoons of the mixture on to the prepared baking sheets, about 5 cm (2 inches) apart to allow for spreading during cooking. Cook in a preheated moderate oven (180°C/ 350°F, Gas Mark 4) for 10 to 15 minutes until lightly golden. Leave to cool on a wire rack.

Melt the chocolate in a bowl over hot water or in a double boiler and coat the undersides of the Florentines. Leave to set in a cool place.
Makes about 6 to 8

Clockwise from front: Chocolate Truffles;
Florentines; Honey Nut Squares (page 56);
Coffee Walnut Creams (page 40);
Viennese Stars (page 62)
(Photograph: Kraft Foods)

Surprise Truffles

METRIC/IMPERIAL
75 g/3 oz full fat soft
    cheese
1 teaspoon milk
100 g/4 oz icing sugar,
    sieved
100 g/4 oz drinking
    chocolate powder
100 g/4 oz cocktail
    cherries
40-50 g/1½-2 oz
    chocolate vermicelli

AMERICAN
⅓ cup full fat soft
    cheese
1 teaspoon milk
1 scant cup sifted
    confectioners'
    sugar
1 cup sifted
    sweetened cocoa
    powder
½ cup cocktail
    cherries
¼ cup chocolate
    sprinkles

Cream the cheese and milk together. Gradually work in the icing (confectioners') sugar and chocolate (cocoa) powder to form a stiff paste. Turn out on to a work surface liberally dusted with icing sugar and roll out to a 5 mm (¼ inch) thickness. Using a 3.5 cm (1½ inch) cutter, cut out 12 rounds.

Rinse and dry the cherries and roll a piece of the chocolate mixture round each to form a smooth ball. Roll each truffle in vermicelli (sprinkles) to coat them. Place in paper sweet (candy) cases.
Makes 12

Chocolate Crisps

METRIC/IMPERIAL
50 g/2 oz butter
40 g/1½ oz caster
    sugar
75 g/3 oz stoned
    dates, chopped
40 g/1½ oz rice cereal
150 g/5 oz chocolate,
    broken into pieces

AMERICAN
¼ cup butter
3 tablespoons sugar
½ cup chopped dates
1½ cups rice cereal
5 squares (1 oz each)
    chocolate, broken
    into pieces

Melt the butter in a pan over a gentle heat. Add the sugar and dates. Remove from the heat and stir in the cereal. Press into a greased 15 cm (6 inch) square tin (pan) and chill.

Melt the chocolate in a bowl over a pan of hot water. Pour the chocolate over the mixture in the tin and chill until set. Cut into 36 squares.
Makes 36

Chocolate Mint Fingers

METRIC/IMPERIAL
Base:
50 g/2 oz
    unsweetened
    chocolate, broken
    into pieces
100 g/4 oz butter
2 eggs
225 g/8 oz sugar
¼ teaspoon
    peppermint
    essence
½ teaspoon salt
100 g/4 oz plain flour
50 g/2 oz flaked
    almonds
Filling:
50 g/2 oz butter
175 g/6 oz icing sugar,
    sieved
1 tablespoon double
    cream
¼ teaspoon
    peppermint
    essence
Topping:
50 g/2 oz
    unsweetened
    chocolate, broken
    into pieces
25 g/1 oz butter

AMERICAN
Base:
2 squares (1 oz each)
    semi-sweet
    chocolate, broken
    into pieces
½ cup butter
2 eggs
1 cup sugar
¼ teaspoon
    peppermint extract
½ teaspoon salt
1 cup all-purpose
    flour
½ cup slivered
    almonds
Filling:
¼ cup butter
1⅓ cups sifted
    confectioners'
    sugar
1 tablespoon heavy
    cream
¼ teaspoon
    peppermint extract
Topping:
2 squares (1 oz each)
    semi-sweet
    chocolate, broken
    into pieces
2 tablespoons butter

First make the base: melt the chocolate and butter in a bowl over a pan of hot water. Whisk the eggs in another bowl until frothy and stir in the sugar, peppermint essence (extract) and chocolate and butter mixture. Add the salt, flour and almonds and mix thoroughly. Pour into a greased 23 cm (9 inch) tin (pan) and cook in a preheated moderate oven (180°C/350°F, Gas Mark 4) for 25 minutes. Leave the base until cold.

To prepare the filling: cream together the butter and icing (confectioners') sugar. Work in the cream and peppermint essence (extract). Spread over the base and chill.

Make the topping by melting the chocolate and butter in a bowl over hot water. Drizzle the topping over the peppermint cream and chill, then cut into 48 fingers.
Makes 48

Tutti-Frutti Truffles

METRIC/IMPERIAL	AMERICAN
75 g/3 oz full fat soft cheese	⅓ cup cream cheese
25 g/1 oz icing sugar, sieved	¼ cup sifted confectioners' sugar
25 g/1 oz glacé cherries, chopped	3 tablespoons chopped glacé cherries
25 g/1 oz angelica, chopped	3 tablespoons chopped angelica
25 g/1 oz seedless raisins, chopped	3 tablespoons chopped raisins
25 g/1 oz hazelnuts, chopped	¼ cup chopped hazelnuts
Decoration:	**Decoration:**
175-225 g (6-8 oz) plain chocolate, broken into pieces	4-6 squares (1 oz each) semi-sweet chocolate, broken into pieces
crystallized rose petals and violets	crystallized rose petals and violets

Cream together the cheese and sugar. Mix in the cherries, angelica, raisins and nuts. Liberally sprinkle the work surface with icing (confectioners') sugar and roll the mixture into 14 balls. Place them on a wire rack with a sheet of waxed paper under the rack.

Melt the chocolate in a bowl over a pan of hot water or in a double boiler. Carefully spoon the melted chocolate over the truffles to coat them. Coat the truffles twice if necessary. Decorate each truffle with crystallized rose petals or violets.
Makes 14

Cherry Truffles

METRIC/IMPERIAL	AMERICAN
175 g/6 oz plain chocolate	6 squares (1 oz each) semi-sweet chocolate
2 tablespoons brandy	2 tablespoons brandy
40 g/1½ oz unsalted butter, softened	3 tablespoons softened unsalted butter
50 g/2 oz icing sugar, sieved	½ cup sifted confectioners' sugar
50 g/2 oz ground almonds	½ cup ground almonds
8 glacé cherries	8 glacé cherries

Melt 100 g/4 oz of the chocolate with the brandy in a bowl over a pan of hot water or in a double boiler. Remove from the heat and stir in the butter, sugar and ground almonds and mix thoroughly. If necessary, leave the mixture in a cold place until firm.

With damp hands, roll the mixture into 16 balls. Grate the remaining chocolate onto greaseproof (waxed) paper and roll the truffles in it. Place each truffle in a paper sweet (candy) case and press half a cherry on top.
Makes 16

Oaty Truffles

METRIC/IMPERIAL	AMERICAN
50 g/2 oz margarine	¼ cup margarine
5 tablespoons milk	⅓ cup milk
75 g/3 oz caster sugar	⅓ cup sugar
25 g/1 oz cocoa powder, sieved	¼ cup sifted unsweetened cocoa powder
100 g/4 oz rolled oats	1 cup rolled oats
100 g/4 oz desiccated coconut	1⅓ cups shredded coconut
25 g/1 oz seedless raisins, chopped	3 tablespoons chopped raisins
chocolate vermicelli to decorate	chocolate sprinkles to decorate

Melt the margarine and milk in a pan over a gentle heat. Beat in the sugar, cocoa, oats, coconut and raisins. Chill the mixture.

With slightly damp hands, form the mixture into 40 balls and roll in the chocolate vermicelli (sprinkles). Place the truffles in paper sweet (candy) cases and chill until set.
Makes 40

All Sorts of Sweets & Candies

In this super selection there are all kinds of new recipe ideas. Many of these sweets and candies use honey as a natural sweetener instead of sugar to give them a pleasant flavour and a chewy texture.

Honeycomb

METRIC/IMPERIAL	AMERICAN
225 g/8 oz soft brown sugar	1⅓ cups light brown sugar
225 g/8 oz granulated sugar	1 cup sugar
50 g/2 oz golden syrup	3 tablespoons light corn syrup
2 tablespoons water	2 tablespoons water
15 g/½ oz butter	1 tablespoon butter
1 tablespoon bicarbonate of soda	1 tablespoon baking soda

Dissolve the sugars and syrup in the water in a large, heavy-based pan over a gentle heat. Boil briskly to the hard crack stage (150°C/300°F). Remove from the heat and stir in the butter, then the soda. Pour immediately into a greased 18 × 28 cm (7 × 11 inch) shallow tin (pan) and leave until cold. Break into about 30 pieces.
Makes about 30

Honey Mallow Crunchies

METRIC/IMPERIAL	AMERICAN
100 g/4 oz marshmallows	4 oz marshmallows
2 tablespoons clear honey	2 tablespoons honey
grated rind of 1 lemon	grated rind of 1 lemon
grated rind of 1 orange	grated rind of 1 orange
75 g/3 oz cornflakes, lightly crushed	3 cups cornflakes, lightly crushed
25 g/1 oz raisins	3 tablespoons raisins

Place the marshmallows and honey in a bowl over a pan of boiling water and stir gently until melted and smooth. Remove from the heat and add the lemon and orange rinds, cereal and raisins and mix thoroughly.

With damp hands, shape the mixture into 30 balls and place each one in a paper sweet (candy) case. Leave to set in a cool place.
Makes 30

Honeycomb; Honey Mallow Crunchies
(Photograph: Tate & Lyle)

Melting Meringues

METRIC/IMPERIAL
1 egg white
50 g/2 oz soft brown
   sugar
25 g/1 oz almonds,
   very finely chopped
1 tablespoon
   chocolate spread
glacé cherry and
   angelica to
   decorate

AMERICAN
1 egg white
⅓ cup light brown
   sugar
¼ cup very finely
   chopped almonds
1 tablespoon
   chocolate spread
glacé cherry and
   angelica to
   decorate

Whisk the egg white until white but still soft. Whisk in half the sugar until stiff. Whisk in remaining sugar until very stiff and fold in the almonds.

Spoon the meringue into a piping (pastry) bag fitted with a star nozzle and pipe 24 stars onto a baking sheet lined with non-stick (parchment) paper. Cook in a preheated very cool oven (120°C/250°F, Gas Mark ½) for 1 hour. Leave until cold.

Sandwich the meringues together in pairs with chocolate spread and decorate with a tiny piece of cherry and angelica. Place in 12 paper sweet (candy) cases.
Makes 12

Honey Nut Squares

METRIC/IMPERIAL
40 g/1½ oz full fat soft
   cheese
1 tablespoon honey
200 g/7 oz icing sugar,
   sieved
40 g/1½ oz nuts,
   chopped and
   toasted
6 glacé cherries,
   chopped
4 dried apricots,
   chopped
To finish:
1 tablespoon
   cornflour
1 tablespoon icing
   sugar

AMERICAN
¼ cup full fat soft
   cheese
1 tablespoon honey
1½ cups sifted
   confectioners'
   sugar
1½ tablespoons
   chopped and
   toasted nuts
6 glacé cherries,
   chopped
4 dried apricots,
   chopped
To finish:
1 tablespoon
   cornstarch
1 tablespoon
   confectioners'
   sugar

Cream the cheese and beat in the honey, sugar, nuts, cherries and apricots.

Sift together the cornflour (cornstarch) and icing (confectioners') sugar and sprinkle half on to the work surface. Spoon the cream cheese mixture on to the work surface. Sprinkle remaining cornflour (cornstarch) mixture on top and shape the mixture into a 15 cm (6 inch) square block. Wrap in non-stick (parchment) paper and chill. Cut into 36 squares and store in the refrigerator.
Makes 36
Illustrated on page 51

Orange and Chocolate Pyramids

METRIC/IMPERIAL
2 egg whites
150 g/5 oz caster
  sugar
150 g/5 oz desiccated
  coconut
finely grated rind of
  1 orange
40 g/1½ oz chopped
  mixed peel
angelica leaves to
  decorate

AMERICAN
2 egg whites
⅔ cup sugar
1⅔ cups shredded
  coconut
finely grated rind of
  1 orange
¼ cup finely chopped
  mixed candied peel
angelica leaves to
  decorate

Line a baking sheet with rice paper. Whisk the egg whites until stiff in a deep bowl. Gradually whisk in the sugar until stiff. Fold in the coconut, orange rind and mixed peel. Using teaspoons, make 20 mounds on the rice paper and place an angelica leaf on top of each.

Cook in a preheated very cool oven (120°C/250°F, Gas Mark ½) for 45 to 60 minutes until light brown. Leave for 3 to 4 hours in a warm place to finish drying out.
Makes 20

Ginger Crispies

METRIC/IMPERIAL
75 g/3 oz butter
50 g/2 oz golden
  syrup
50 g/2 oz light brown
  sugar
1 tablespoon milk
1 teaspoon ground
  ginger
75 g/3 oz rice cereal
angelica leaves to
  decorate

AMERICAN
¼ cup plus
  2 tablespoons butter
3 tablespoons light
  corn syrup
⅓ cup light brown
  sugar
1 tablespoon milk
1 teaspoon ground
  ginger
3 cups rice cereal
angelica leaves to
  decorate

Melt the butter, syrup, sugar, milk and ginger in a deep pan over a gentle heat. Bring to the boil and boil for 3 minutes. Remove from the heat and mix in the cereal.

Spoon the mixture into 36 paper sweet (candy) cases. Decorate with the angelica leaves. Leave to set in a cold place.
Makes 36

Peanut Chews

METRIC/IMPERIAL
75 g/3 oz margarine
6 tablespoons thick
  honey
225 g/8 oz digestive
  biscuits, crushed
4 tablespoons
  crunchy peanut
  butter

AMERICAN
¼ cup plus
  2 tablespoons
  margarine
6 tablespoons thick
  honey
2 cups graham
  cracker crumbs
¼ cup crunchy
  peanut butter

Melt the margarine in a pan over a gentle heat. Add the honey and stir continuously until the mixture comes to the boil. Remove from the heat. Stir in the biscuit (cracker) crumbs and peanut butter. Press the mixture into a greased 18 cm (7 inch) square tin (pan) and chill. Cut into 36 squares.
Makes 36

Jumble Roll

METRIC/IMPERIAL
225 g/8 oz stoned
  dates, chopped
100 g/4 oz walnuts,
  chopped
75 g/3 oz glacé
  cherries, chopped
225 g/8 oz sweet
  biscuits, crushed
125 g/5 oz
  marshmallows,
  snipped into pieces
150 ml/¼ pint
  evaporated milk

AMERICAN
1⅓ cups chopped
  dates
1 cup chopped
  walnuts
⅓ cup chopped glacé
  cherries
2 cups graham
  cracker crumbs
5 oz marshmallows,
  snipped into pieces
⅔ cup evaporated
  milk

Mix the dates, walnuts, cherries, biscuit (cracker) crumbs and marshmallows with enough of the milk to make a moist mixture which sticks together. Form into a long roll on waxed paper. Wrap up tightly and chill overnight. Cut into slices to serve.
Makes about 40

Honey Nut Clusters

METRIC/IMPERIAL	AMERICAN
225 g/8 oz ginger biscuits	½ lb ginger cookies
4 tablespoons clear honey	4 tablespoons honey
75 g/3 oz margarine	¼ cup plus 2 tablespoons margarine
50 g/2 oz walnuts, chopped	½ cup chopped walnuts
50 g/2 oz chopped mixed peel	⅓ cup chopped candied peel
50 g/2 oz glacé cherries, chopped	¼ cup chopped glacé cherries
50 g/2 oz raisins	⅓ cup raisins

Place the ginger biscuits (cookies) in a bag and crush them to crumbs using a rolling pin.

Melt the honey and margarine in a pan over a gentle heat. Remove from the heat. Stir in the walnuts, peel, crumbs, cherries and raisins. Form the mixture into 12 balls and place in paper sweet (candy) cases.
Makes 12

Mini Macaroons

METRIC/IMPERIAL	AMERICAN
2 egg whites	2 egg whites
100 g/4 oz caster sugar	½ cup sugar
75 g/3 oz ground almonds	¾ cup ground almonds
50 g/2 oz plain chocolate	⅓ cup chocolate chips

Whisk the egg whites until stiff, then whisk in the sugar a little at a time. Fold in the ground almonds with a metal spoon.

Spoon the mixture into a piping (pastry) bag fitted with a 1 cm (½ inch) plain nozzle and pipe the mixture on to a lightly oiled baking sheet in about 4 cm (1½ inch) lengths. Cook in a preheated cool oven (140°C/275°F, Gas Mark 1) for 1 to 1½ hours. Leave for a few minutes, then transfer to a wire rack and leave to cool.

Melt the chocolate in a bowl over a pan of hot water and dip the ends of the macaroons into the chocolate. Leave on non-stick (parchment) paper until set.
Makes about 45

Chocolate Crispy Squares

METRIC/IMPERIAL	AMERICAN
2 tablespoons clear honey	2 tablespoons honey
25 g/1 oz margarine	2 tablespoons margarine
100 g/4 oz icing sugar, sieved	1 scant cup sifted confectioners' sugar
50 g/2 oz cornflakes	2 cups cornflakes
2 teaspoons instant coffee granules, mixed with 1 teaspoon hot water	2 teaspoons instant coffee granules, mixed with 1 teaspoon hot water
100 g/4 oz chocolate dots	⅔ cup semi-sweet chocolate morsels

Melt the honey and margarine in a large pan over a gentle heat. Remove from the heat. Stir in the sugar, cornflakes and coffee. Press the mixture into a greased 15 cm (6 inch) square tin (pan) and chill.

Melt the chocolate in a bowl over a pan of hot water or in a double boiler. Pour the chocolate over the cold mixture in the tin and chill. Cut into 36 squares.
Makes 36

Chocolate Crispy Squares; Honey Nut Clusters;
Coconut Kisses (page 60)
(Photograph: Gales Honey Bureau)

Coconut Kisses

METRIC/IMPERIAL
175 g/6 oz desiccated
  coconut
3 tablespoons clear
  honey
1 egg white
pink food colouring

AMERICAN
2 cups shredded
  coconut
3 tablespoons honey
1 egg white
pink food coloring

Mix the coconut, honey and egg white in a bowl to form a stiff paste. Divide in half and colour one portion pink. Make 10 balls out of each colour mixture and arrange on a baking tray lined with non-stick (parchment) paper.

Dry out the sweets (candies) in a very cool oven (120°C/250°F, Gas Mark ½) for about 15 minutes. Leave until cold, then place in paper sweet (candy) cases.
Makes 20
Illustrated on page 59

Tiffin

METRIC/IMPERIAL
100 g/4 oz margarine
2 tablespoons golden
  syrup
2 tablespoons caster
  sugar
225 g/8 oz sweet
  biscuits, crushed
25 g/1 oz cocoa
  powder, sieved
100 g/4 oz mixed
  dried fruit
225 g/8 oz chocolate,
  broken into pieces

AMERICAN
½ cup margarine
2 tablespoons light
  corn syrup
2 tablespoons sugar
2 cups graham
  cracker crumbs
¼ cup sifted
  unsweetened cocoa
  powder
⅔ cup mixed dried
  fruit
8 squares (1 oz each)
  chocolate, broken
  into pieces

Melt the margarine, syrup and sugar in a pan over a gentle heat. Remove from the heat and stir in the biscuit (cracker) crumbs, cocoa and fruit. Pour into a greased 15 cm (6 inch) square tin (pan) and press down. Chill.

Melt the chocolate in a bowl over a pan of hot water or in a double boiler and pour over the cold mixture. Decorate the top with a fork and leave until set. Cut into 36 squares.
Makes 36

Peppermint Slices

METRIC/IMPERIAL
Base:
100 g/4 oz block
  margarine
2 teaspoons cocoa,
  sieved
100 g/4 oz plain flour,
  sieved
65 g/2½ oz
  cornflakes, crushed
75 g/3 oz soft brown
  sugar
Filling:
225 g/8 oz icing sugar,
  sieved
2 tablespoons water
½ teaspoon
  peppermint
  essence
few drops of green
  food colouring
Topping:
150 g/5 oz chocolate,
  broken into pieces

AMERICAN
Base:
½ cup margarine
2 teaspoons sifted
  unsweetened cocoa
  powder
1 cup sifted
  all-purpose flour
2½ cups crushed
  cornflakes
½ cup light brown
  sugar
Filling:
1¾ cups sifted
  confectioners'
  sugar
2 tablespoons water
½ teaspoon
  peppermint extract
few drops of green
  food coloring
Topping:
5 squares (1 oz each)
  semi-sweet
  chocolate, broken
  into pieces

To make the base: melt the margarine in a pan over a gentle heat. Stir in the cocoa, flour, cornflakes and brown sugar. Pour into a greased 28 × 18 cm (11 × 7 inch) Swiss roll tin (jelly roll pan) and press down. Cook in a preheated moderate oven (180°C/350°F, Gas Mark 4) for 15 to 20 minutes. Leave in the tin until cold.

Make the filling by mixing the sugar, water, peppermint and colouring together to make a stiff icing. Spread over the base and chill for 30 minutes.

Melt the chocolate in a bowl over a pan of hot water. Remove from the heat and leave to cool. Spoon the melted chocolate over the set icing to cover it completely. Reserve some chocolate and pipe a pretty design on top when the chocolate cover is hard. Cut into 48 slices.
Makes 48

Fruity Clusters

METRIC/IMPERIAL	AMERICAN
15 g/½ oz butter	1 tablespoon butter
2 tablespoons golden syrup	2 tablespoons light corn syrup
50 g/2 oz almonds, chopped	½ cup chopped almonds
50 g/2 oz glacé cherries, chopped	¼ cup chopped glacé cherries
100 g/4 oz chopped mixed peel	⅔ cup chopped candied peel
75 g/3 oz raisins, chopped	½ cup chopped raisins
1 teaspoon lemon juice	1 teaspoon lemon juice

Melt the butter and syrup in a pan over a gentle heat. Boil the mixture until it turns golden brown.

Put the almonds, cherries, mixed peel, raisins and lemon juice in a large bowl. Pour the syrup mixture on to the fruit and nuts and chill. When nearly set, place teaspoons of the mixture into 20 paper sweet (candy) cases and leave to set.
Makes 20
Illustrated on page 43

Chocolate Chews

METRIC/IMPERIAL	AMERICAN
50 g/2 oz margarine	¼ cup margarine
25 g/1 oz sugar	2 tablespoons sugar
4 tablespoons sweetened condensed milk	¼ cup sweetened condensed milk
100 g/4 oz rolled oats	1 cup rolled oats
50 g/2 oz desiccated coconut	⅔ cup shredded coconut
25 g/1 oz drinking chocolate powder	¼ cup sweetened cocoa powder

Melt the margarine and sugar in a pan over a gentle heat. Stir in the milk, rolled oats, coconut and drinking chocolate (cocoa) powder and mix thoroughly.

Spoon into a well greased 15 cm (6 inch) square tin (pan) and level the surface. Cook in a preheated moderate oven (180°C/350°F, Gas Mark 4) for about 30 minutes. Cut into 36 squares while warm. Leave in the tin until cold.
Makes 36

Crunchy Coffee Surprises

METRIC/IMPERIAL	AMERICAN
Base:	**Base:**
25 g/1 oz butter	2 tablespoons butter
3 tablespoons golden syrup	3 tablespoons light corn syrup
50 g/2 oz rice cereal	2 cups rice cereal
1 tablespoon desiccated coconut	1 tablespoon shredded coconut
Filling:	**Filling:**
1 teaspoon instant coffee	1 teaspoon instant coffee
1 teaspoon hot water	1 teaspoon hot water
18 large marshmallows	18 large marshmallows
1 small banana, sliced	1 small banana, sliced
Decoration:	**Decoration:**
chocolate vermicelli	chocolate sprinkles

To make the base: melt the butter and syrup in a pan over a gentle heat. Bring to the boil and boil gently for 1 minute. Stir in the rice cereal and coconut. Spoon the mixture into 12 paper cake cases and press gently over the bases and up the sides to line the cases. Chill.

Dissolve the coffee in the water in a bowl over a pan of hot water or in a double boiler. Add the marshmallows and stir until melted. Put a slice of banana in each case and cover with the marshmallow mixture. Leave to set. Sprinkle with chocolate vermicelli (sprinkles).
Makes 12

Candy Cushions

METRIC/IMPERIAL	AMERICAN
150 g/5 oz marshmallows	5 oz marshmallows
4 tablespoons milk	¼ cup milk
50 g/2 oz caster sugar	¼ cup sugar
50 g/2 oz butter	¼ cup butter
100 g/4 oz icing sugar, sieved	1 cup sifted confectioners' sugar
50 g/2 oz hazelnuts, chopped	½ cup chopped hazelnuts

Place the marshmallows and 2 tablespoons of the milk in a pan over a gentle heat and melt the marshmallows slowly. Meanwhile, put the remaining milk, caster sugar and butter into another pan and bring to the boil, stirring well. Cook for 5 minutes without stirring.

Remove the milk mixture from the heat and stir in the melted marshmallows, icing (confectioners') sugar and nuts. Pour into a well greased 15 cm (6 inch) square tin (pan) and leave until cold. When hardened, cut into 36 squares.

Makes 36

Cornflake Nests

METRIC/IMPERIAL	AMERICAN
50 g/2 oz butter	¼ cup butter
125 g/5 oz marshmallows	5 oz marshmallows
100 g/4 oz cornflakes	4 cups cornflakes
40 mini eggs	40 mini eggs

Melt the butter and marshmallows in a deep pan over a gentle heat. Remove from the heat and stir in the cornflakes.

Divide the mixture between 40 paper sweet (candy) cases, pressing it together and making a slight hollow in the centre. Leave until cold. Place an egg in each nest.

Makes 40

Viennese Stars

METRIC/IMPERIAL	AMERICAN
100 g/4 oz soft margarine	½ cup soft margarine
25 g/1 oz icing sugar, sieved	¼ cup sifted confectioners' sugar
75 g/3 oz plain flour, sieved	¾ cup sifted all-purpose flour
25 g/1 oz cornflour	¼ cup cornstarch
few drops of vanilla essence	few drops of vanilla
glacé cherries to decorate	glacé cherries to decorate

Cream the margarine and icing (confectioners') sugar together until pale. Mix in the flour, cornflour (cornstarch) and vanilla. Spoon the mixture into a piping (pastry) bag fitted with a 1 cm (½ inch) star nozzle. Pipe tiny stars on to a greased baking sheet and top each with a tiny piece of cherry.

Cook in a preheated moderately hot oven (190°C/375°F, Gas Mark 5) for about 10 minutes until lightly golden. Transfer to a wire rack and leave until cold.

Makes about 24

Illustrated on page 51

Index